THE **POWER** OF PRESENTATION

# TESTIMONIALS

A clear differentiator in leadership is the ability to craft a clear, compelling presentation that motivates and inspires the audience to take a necessary action, or change a behavior. In *The Power of Presentation*, Tommy Re has expertly designed the HINT method to enable everyone to take their presentations of every type to the next level.

**Greg Megowan, EdD, MBA**
*Director, Commercial Training*
*Neurelis*

This book is more than a how-to for effective presentations. It is the WHY presentations are important and how powerful presentations can make significant changes. Tommy provides a valuable road map in a way that can easily be used as a handy reminder of what is important in connecting with your audience. Take a HINT ... this book is sensible and immediately useful.

**Charline S. Russo, EdD**
*Senior Lecturer, Organizational Dynamics, University of Pennsylvania*

Tommy Re has done a great job of delivering a message that is so often overlooked in business: "How you deliver the message will form the audience's reaction to the message." Additionally, *The Power of Presentation* gives the reader a road map on how to deliver while taking the stress out that we all suffer from. And his use of relatable characters makes for an easy, relatable read.

**John Reeves**
*CEO, Microporous*

When a pitch-perfect message and team alignment have been mission critical for me and our company, Tommy has given us all his knowledge, experience, and passion contained in this book, ensuring our success. I'm so excited that he has distilled these qualities into book form for people who aren't as fortunate as I have been to have had him by my side and helping me deliver time and again.

I can confidently say I will keep a copy close by at all times, a wonderful reminder of what he's taught me and quick reference whenever that moment of critical communication should arise.

**Brett Howell**
*CEO, 4th Down Solutions*

Tommy Re has written a masterclass in how to develop and deliver presentations. An idea is worthless unless it is presented properly; *The Power of Presentation* will enable you to get your ideas across powerfully and influence action. For business leaders this is a must read. Practical, pragmatic, focused with instantly actionable tools, techniques, and guidance to inspire your team to achieve high value outcomes.

**David Mantica**
*VP and General Manager, SoftEd US*
*President, DTM Services LLC*

Presenting effectively is one of the keys to career advancement. Don't wait to learn how to do it well. Let Tommy show you how.

**Tamara Ziegler**
*Director, Global Talent Development & Training*
*Worldwide Clinical Trials*

# the **POWER** of PRESENTATION

## A vital GUIDE TO DELIVERING
## COMPELLING BUSINESS PRESENTATIONS

### INTRODUCING THE HINT™ METHOD

# TOMMY RE

### with Taylor De La Pena

*Advantage*®

Published by Advantage, Charleston, South Carolina.
Member of Advantage Media Group.

ADVANTAGE is a registered trademark, and the Advantage colophon is a trademark of Advantage Media Group, Inc.

Printed in the United States of America.

10  9  8  7  6  5  4  3  2  1

ISBN: 978-1-64225-252-1
LCCN: 2022912182

Cover design by Megan Elger.
Layout design by Matthew Morse.
Illustrations by Alyssa D'Avanzo

This publication is designed to provide accurate and authoritative information in regard to the subject matter covered. It is sold with the understanding that the publisher is not engaged in rendering legal, accounting, or other professional services. If legal advice or other expert assistance is required, the services of a competent professional person should be sought.

Advantage Media Group is a publisher of business, self-improvement, and professional development books and online learning. We help entrepreneurs, business leaders, and professionals share their Stories, Passion, and Knowledge to help others Learn & Grow. Do you have a manuscript or book idea that you would like us to consider for publishing? Please visit **advantagefamily.com**.

*For my mother and father —*
*for all the sacrifices you made to educate the four of us.*

# Contents

# Introduction

Places, please!

*— Every stage manager in every theater before every performance*

Presentations have power. They have the power to influence, to inspire, to rally. They even have the power to save lives. Hey! While that might seem a little dramatic, it's true. A well-done and engaging presentation can ensure no one is harmed. Imagine that you work in a laboratory with potentially dangerous chemicals. If there were a real emergency with those chemicals, the safety presentation given by the head of the department might be the most important one you've ever attended. And it would be in that department head's best interest that nobody falls asleep during the presentation that conveys vital safety information. When life or death is on the line, a presentation like this can equip us with the information we need to prevent disaster.

Presentations have the power to cause change. The chief executive officer of an underperforming company develops and presents a new strategy to the board of directors at their organization. Their presentation convinces the board to support a different strategy and becomes the catalyst that transforms the business for the better. Presentations teach us. Think back to the initial training session for your first job.

That presentation invariably shaped the way you started your career and led you to where you are today—for better or worse!

Presentations open minds and spark creativity. Maybe you've been working on a research project that has the potential to provide a huge breakthrough for your field. But you need financial support to get it across the finish line. You present your research, package your ideas, and pitch to key investors. Your inspiring presentation lands you the funding you need to do your vital work. Presentations inspire us. Presentations connect us. Presentations reassure us.

But presentations also have the power to put us to sleep. They can confuse us in a key decision-making moment or make us run from a potential investment or wonder about working at that new company. A presentation can be like the proverbial double-edged sword: wielded correctly, its power is unstoppable, but used incorrectly, it can wound the presenter. Ultimately, the power of your presentation resides in you. Your mind, your eyes, and your voice determine what kind of power your presentation can have over your listeners. For it to have the power you want, you must be in command of all these elements and use them to your advantage. In this book, you will learn how to deliver compelling presentations that influence, inform, and inspire your listeners.

For my whole life, I've been fascinated with how words, images, and voices come together to make things happen. It's maybe for this reason that I chose theater as my first profession. It's such a robust form of communication that can have a huge impact on its audiences. Early in my career, I was fortunate enough to work as a professional actor and playwright in New York City. I even had the great honor of performing in the 1975 Broadway production of *A Chorus Line*. That show would go on to win nine Tony Awards, one of the highest honors in American theater. My time working in the rehearsal studio and acting on the stage gave me an opportunity to explore both sides of the theater—creating and performing. There, I learned how to craft compelling messages and engage my audiences with passionate delivery. I didn't know it then, but I later discovered that these are the two keys to powerful business presentations.

Since I left the theater, I've spent the last thirty years in the field of training and organizational communication. When I ask participants in our sessions to describe presentation skills, they usually respond with a list of platform skills—how to speak in front of a crowd. They want to learn how to be more engaging, be less monotone, or calm their anxiety of speaking in public. But what they come to discover in our training is that's only half the equation. Successful communication requires both a compelling message and a fluent delivery. Throughout this book, we will work on both: the development of your message and the skills you need for a memorable delivery. You'll come to realize that the two go hand in hand. A great message delivered poorly is as unsuccessful as a weak message delivered well.

The theater helped me realize the reason presentations are so effective—because they allow for live discourse. In an increasingly digitized world, both theater and presentations raise the following questions: Why do it live? Why not just make a movie or write a book instead of performing a play? Why is a presentation a better method of communication than a written report in certain situations? Anyone who appreciates live theater will tell you it's about being in the same place at the same time—together—experiencing something with each other that is happening in the moment. Being able to turn to the person next to you and say, "Did you just see or hear or feel that?" This

> **A great message delivered poorly is as unsuccessful as a weak message delivered well.**

impulse has been drawing us together since the first time someone stood up and told a story around a fire.

That's the allure of "doing it live"; a story is unfolding in front of us. This joint experience creates reciprocity: the audience gives feedback, and those on stage respond to it. In the theater we have what's called the "fourth wall," an imaginary veil that separates the onstage action from the audience. But make no mistake—actors feel and sense how the audience is responding even when they are immersed in their roles. It is interactive. It is live. It is dynamic. And it can cause conversations to happen. Presentations in the business world mirror this "in the moment" quality. They might be less dramatic, but in conference halls and meeting rooms, people are gaining new information, having important discussions, and making key decisions—together.

Theater productions and presentations both exist to communicate something vital to an audience. While most might attend a play to be entertained, a good theater production will impart an idea, share a feeling, or inspire its audience to action. Similarly, presentations have specific purposes. We'll go more in depth into these purposes in the next chapter, but to put it simply, presentations can have three potential purposes: to inform, to persuade, or to inspire their audiences. Using my experience in the theater, I've developed an easy-to-learn method for understanding how to structure a presentation that effectively communicates your message to your audience in a way that is just as vital and entertaining as a great play.

And just as Broadway plays won't succeed if they're not meticulously written, cast, and rehearsed, so too will business presentations fail without the proper preparation, development, and delivery. Unlike in theater, though, most people delivering presentations have had little to no formal training or coaching on performing or speaking in public. Which is unfortunate, because presentations form such a vital part of how we communicate with one another in business settings. That's why I've written this book: to use my experience, both as a corporate communication expert and as an experienced performer, to give you the tools you need to take the presentation stage and make it yours.

## The Ensemble

One of the things I love most about theater is that it allows us to learn something important about ourselves through our ability to relate to fictional characters. The most successful plays are those with believable, likeable, and interesting characters whom we want to succeed and overcome the conflicts they face. So, to illustrate the vital components of making presentations, I'm going to use characters who are going through the exact same types of scenarios you might be facing. We'll watch as they fall prey to common pitfalls and then effectively use my process to deliver powerful business presentations.

These characters are composites of the many wonderful professionals I've trained and worked with throughout my career, many of whom have gone on to become senior leaders in their organizations. Through each character, we will explore different aspects of preparing and delivering professional presentations. Each person has a different purpose and a different level of presenting experience, which will allow you to better understand issues you might face and how you can address them. Just as you'll find in the beginning of a play's script, here's a short introduction to each character for your reference. Time to meet our players!

**Chuck** is a project manager working at a clinical trials company. His manager has asked him to give a presentation on the progress of an important clinical trial. While Chuck is an excellent project manager, he doesn't like to speak in public. Nevertheless, the critical nature of this study requires that he keep the executives informed on its progress so they can make pressing decisions. He needs help with crafting his message to convey information succinctly yet memorably.

**Amanda** is an account executive at a major consulting firm. Part of her job is to develop new business, so she spends a good deal of her time pitching—presenting capabilities and solutions to clients who are considering which firm to hire or which solution to adopt. She has an important presentation scheduled soon to persuade members of a prospective executive team to select her firm for a major engagement.

Finally, **Cheryl** is a seasoned consumer products sales manager who has recently been promoted to a director-level role leading a large business unit. She has a lot of experience with giving sales presentations to potential new clients, and while she is very good at that task, this new role will require her to inspire her large team. This new role will require Cheryl to give thought-provoking and meaningful presentations on the main stage at national company meetings—an audience and content area she's never experienced before.

As we explore the presentation challenges each character faces, I'll lay out the ideas, tools, and exercises they can use to develop and deliver their presentations. And, not to worry, you'll get those exact same resources to hone your own presentation skills. Each section of the book will end with key takeaways that will provide you with your own practice opportunities in this vital skill. You can find any tools I reference in this book online at www.talentisvital.com.

In my life as a Broadway performer, the last thing I'd hear before hitting the stage would be the phrase "Places, please!" It's a clarion call to performers to ready themselves to take the spotlight and start the show. In all my years as a professional actor, these two words never failed to generate excitement. I lived for that moment of focus those words would bring and the anticipation it stirred within me before stepping onstage to bring the story to life and connect with my audience. So, "Places, please!" Get ready to work on that important presentation of yours so that when it's your turn to take to the stage, you'll shine.

PART 1

# DEVELOPING YOUR PRESENTATION

# CHAPTER 1

# The Guiding Principles

We should be as careful of our words as of our actions.

—*Cicero*

If you want to create and deliver compelling business presentations, you've got to learn to play a few different roles. At times, you'll play the role of writer—conducting rigorous research like a journalist, crafting your opinion like an editorialist, or understanding your topic like a textbook writer. Other times, you'll play the role of a designer who works on the visual impact of your presentation, tweaking slide decks and adding videos to capture the attention of your audience. Finally, you'll need to become the actor (and for some, this is the most challenging role) when you deliver your presentation with confidence and enthusiasm. When you give that presentation, you'll be on some type of stage. It might be a real stage at a conference, the front of the meeting room, or the center of attention on a web conference call, but an audience will be there watching and listening. These three roles—writer, actor, and designer—correspond to the three guiding principles we'll use throughout this book. They are simple and are designed to help you stay focused.

The first principle is that **presentations put your thinking on display**. In most business communication, your audience is interested in the quality of your thinking. For instance, they might want to know why your product is better than that of the competitors, why the company earnings are below estimates, or how you plan to restructure manufacturing operations to meet growing demand. This is where you'll play the role of writer. Like a writer, you'll need to structure your ideas into crisp messages. I like to say that good communicators make the vague clear, the abstract concrete, and the complex simple. They do this so that their audiences can easily digest the information they deliver.

The second principle is that **presentations are a multichannel communication experience**. In a presentation, you are combining verbal, nonverbal, and visual communication. Throughout this book, I'll show you that great presentations rely equally on the quality of the visuals and the quality of the words. In fact, according to the dual coding theory developed by Allan Paivio in 1986, the brain processes information using two primary channels: verbal and visual. When both modes are working together, the brain creates a library of words and images with a mental cross-reference between them. This helps you remember and recall better. This dual system of processing and storage explains why memorized information is more likely to be retrieved when it is stored in both visual and verbal form.

> **Good communicators make the vague clear, the abstract concrete, and the complex simple.**

Good presenters must think like designers. If you want to make sure your audience can easily recall the information in your presentation, make sure you incorporate graphics associated with text or use an audio track with an animation. Placing pictures together with words also allows these two modes of information to form connections in the minds of your audience members. These connections are called schemas, and they help us remember what's important and what's not. The minute you put up a slide, your audience's attention is focused only on what you've put on the screen. Immediately they'll start trying to make connections between the visuals on the screen and the words that you are saying. So, the design of your presentation needs to be well thought out and support—not detract from—your message.

Third, **your platform skills matter**. Let's face it: a presentation is a type of performance. That's the reality whether we like it or not. If you are unable to deliver your message fluently and convincingly, your presentation won't be successful. So, here you'll need to play the role of actor. Actors take stories and bring them to life. You will need to bring your story to life when you deliver your presentation. Later in the book, I'll show you how to prepare the way actors do and how you can use the psychology of performance to your benefit and, perhaps more importantly, to your audience's benefit.

We'll keep these three principles in mind throughout the journey to powerful presentations. This book is a guide that takes you step by step through the presentation process, from putting together your slide deck until the moment you're ready to deliver it. You can certainly jump around for tips on various aspects of presenting, but if you want to learn a proven, repeatable process, go chapter by chapter and keep your own presentation situation in mind.

# Chapter 1 Key Takeaways

- Presentations are a way to put your thinking on display for your colleagues. This open line of communication helps people make decisions, collaborate over problems, and learn vital information for their daily work.
- Presentations are multichannel experiences where an audience gets the chance to digest information in two different ways— through a well-constructed talk track and carefully considered visuals.
- Being a good presenter isn't just about talking over a slide deck. You'll need to think like a communicator and a designer to effectively communicate your message to your audiences.

# CHAPTER 2

# Respond to the Communication Situation

To ask the right question is already half the solution of a problem.

—*Carl Jung*

Your boss sends you an email that reads, "The executive team needs an update on how we're progressing on the new compensation plan. Can you put a presentation together by Friday so we can meet with them next week?" Or you've just learned that your firm has made it to the final two vendors for a major new contract, and the customer has asked you to prepare a bid defense. Maybe you recently got a promotion to a senior leadership role in your organization, and you need to address the company and talk about your vision for the future. All these instances are unique communication situations that require you to navigate how people exchange big ideas and tactical strategies with each other.

Communication situations arise in business every day. They are made up of two important elements. The first is something that needs attention—either a problem that needs to be solved or an opportunity that needs to be developed. The second important element of a communication situation is an audience or the people who are impacted by the situation. Not all communication situations require a presentation—sometimes they can be solved by an email. But every presentation is **a response** to a communication situation. When you are creating your own presentation, you need to explore both elements in detail. They are imperative to delivering a presentation with impact.

## Why Presentations?

But why a presentation? Wouldn't a memo or email do? Think of it this way: Can you imagine someone handing out the best man's toast at a wedding and asking the guests to read it silently? Or sending your new team a memo to introduce yourself and discuss team goals, norms, and expectations? Not a great way to build team cohesion.

> **Presentations are opportunities to teach, influence, celebrate, and, in business, get things done.**

Presentations are opportunities to teach, influence, celebrate, and, in business, get things done. They are occasions when we embrace the spoken word and the listening audience to help accomplish something worthwhile. And we do it live. Together.

So that we have a shared understanding, let's define presentations in detail. A presentation is a live oral public communication. What does that mean? Let's break it down further:

- **Live**—It might be virtual or face to face, but it's happening right now in this moment. It's not recorded. It might be broadcast to be viewed later, but a live presentation is done once, and there are no do-overs. This "in the moment" aspect is key to presentations, and it's a quality that can hang up a lot of presenters. The liveness adds an element of tension, but it's also what makes it exciting.

- **Oral**—This aspect is about the audience. They get to hear the presenter speak. A presentation is not a document or Slidedoc—a document created in PowerPoint that could be read and completely understood without a speaker. It might be accompanied by both, but these documents only supplement the presentation.
- **Public**—In general, presentations are a one-to-many form of communication. In contrast, one-to-one communication is called interpersonal communication. Although some business presentations are for one person (updating your boss on a project, for example), most are given to groups.

## The Benefits of Presentations

Presentations matter in organizations because they not only communicate important information but also help clarify understanding and facilitate immediate dialogue and decision-making.

### THEY HELP CLARIFY UNDERSTANDING

Have you ever read a document and thought, *What is the author trying to say here?* In written communication, you can't hear the subtle nuance in a speaker's voice that allows for a better understanding of the message. You can't see facial expressions, body movements, or gestures that provide clues to understanding. You are not able to give feedback—not immediately, anyway. While written communication is important, verbal communication provides a wider range of options, such as nonverbal cues like gestures and eye contact, that make a presentation a powerful opportunity to ensure common understanding.

## THEY FACILITATE IMMEDIATE DIALOGUE AND DECISION-MAKING

Perhaps the most important selling point for live presentations is their immediacy. A presentation is an opportunity for immediate discussion and debate about its topic. Written documents require that everyone reads them—which often means that not everyone does. And it's impossible to have a robust and inclusive discussion when some participants don't have a full understanding of the topic. With presentations, all attendees receive the same information at the same time, making it much easier to hold a discussion or debate. And if a decision needs to be made, the relevant information and opinions will already have been shared. Live presentations make decision-making easier and more efficient. As you prepare your presentations, think about how to leverage these distinctive aspects of live presentations.

In the next two chapters we're going to look at what needs your attention—we'll call this **the mission**—and **the audience** that you'll be presenting to. Both are integral to your response. Let's start with the mission.

# Chapter 2 Key Takeaways

- A communication situation is any situation in which you must address an audience to resolve an issue with certain constraints. Your presentation is a response to this communication situation.
- Presentations are live, oral, and public. They're one of the most popular one-to-many communication styles.
- The benefits of giving a presentation include the ability to use nonverbal cues and visual media to clarify your message. They also facilitate immediate discussion and decision-making.

CHAPTER 3

# Know Your Mission

A good archer is known not by his arrows, but by his aim.

—*Thomas Fuller*

As we said earlier, your presentation is a response to a communication situation. This is comprised of two things: something that needs to be addressed, either a problem or an opportunity, and the audience, the people involved in the situation. What communication situations do you find yourself in? Think about the different presentations you're asked to give at work. What are you being asked to do, and what are you trying to accomplish? If you look critically at most presentations at work, your mission will typically fall into three categories. As we explore these categories, we'll work alongside three characters: Chuck, Amanda, and Cheryl. Each character has a high-stakes presentation coming up where their mission will fall into one of these categories. You'll watch them shape their presentations and get them ready for delivery. You'll learn about the challenges they face in developing their presentations, including some common pitfalls associated with each type of presentation. In subsequent chapters, we'll use these characters' experiences to explore how you can navigate the challenges that arise in your communication situation.

The first are **presentations that inform**. In these presentations, you've got to explain something to your audience, like how a process in your department works or why sales are down for one of your products. The second category is **presentations that persuade**. In these kinds of presentations, you need to persuade someone to take an action. Maybe you want them to buy something or agree to your proposed approach to a project. Finally in our list are **presentations that inspire**. Let's say you need to touch the hearts of a group and move them to action. Through a presentation that inspires, you will lift them up and help them tackle a tough challenge, like taking on the competition or making their way through a difficult change. These kinds of presentations can have powerful ramifications on your people.

Can't pinpoint your presentation to one category? That's just fine. The truth is, most presentations are a combination of all three. Think of these three high-level presentation purposes as dials. Your job is to dial in the right amount of each to achieve your goal. How you make those choices is essentially your **communication strategy**. If your purpose is primarily to persuade, there are some specific tactics you can use to do that. There are also some pitfalls to watch out for too. Each purpose brings its own set of challenges that we want to be aware of. Let's take a look at some tactics that will help you deliver a purposeful presentation with real impact.

## The Most Common Communication Situations

### PRESENTATIONS THAT INFORM

We get lots of opportunity to explain things at work. That's because everyone wants to know how things are going and what situations they need to be prepared for. It's that quarterly business review that shapes what actions will need to be taken in the next quarter. Or it's an update at a shareholder meeting that affects day-to-day operations within an organization. Or a project status meeting that can impact every client deliverable that team members work on. Training, customer education, and onboarding situations are also chock full of information that needs to be passed from one party to another. Information moves businesses and organizations forward. Knowing how to impart it through a presentation is an invaluable skill for anyone who wants to get things done.

The goal is to impart information to the audience so they can do something with it, like make a decision, take action, or change something. Developing and delivering a presentation designed to explain something can be challenging. They can be dry, they can be boring, and they can be long and unwieldy. And when that happens, they will not even achieve the simplest objective of any communication—to get people to pay attention.

## MEET CHUCK

### *Chuck Reinmann, Project Manager, Clinical Trials at Excel Biotech*

Chuck is a project manager working on an important clinical trial that may change the course of treatment for severe mental illness. The study has gotten off to a good start but is now experiencing some difficulties. The senior leadership team is anxious to hear from Chuck regarding the most recent status of the project and the implications for the company.

Chuck's presentation purpose at the highest level is to inform. He needs to explain where the project is, what problems he's having, and what he plans to do to get the project back on track. Ultimately, his presentation is meant to help his audience gain intelligence about the project and be prepared to make future decisions. Now, while Chuck is a great project manager, he really doesn't like speaking in public. He knows, however, that communicating the study's status is an important part of his job. He also understands that this presentation is not like most of the others that he gives on a routine basis. This is a high-stakes, high-profile presentation.

## THE CHALLENGES WITH INFORMING

Presentations that inform are a mainstay of corporate communication. They come in many forms: technical presentations, training sessions, project updates, and financial and operating reports. They rely on accuracy and clarity. They often require the presenter to synthesize information and make decisions about what information is relevant and how it should be prioritized.

There are three common pitfalls with this type of presentation. The first is the one I mentioned earlier: these presentations require communicating technical information, which by its nature can be dry. This can lead to **presentations that bore the audience**. It's unlikely that in the business world you'll see people sleeping, but you might see people multitasking, checking phones or email, or maybe daydreaming. They might be physically awake, but mentally they are asleep. If their frustration level starts to rise with a bad informational presentation, you'll start to see fidgeting behavior—tapping feet, glancing at watches, and appearing restless.

The second is **information overload**, which is also known as data dumping. This is when a presenter's delivery of facts and figures overwhelms the audience because it's not structured properly. Data that doesn't lead to insights is useless to decision makers. When data is not structured and synthesized by the presenter, it puts too much cognitive load on the audience. You've basically asked them to do your job, on the spot and without the luxury of time to organize the information. Remember, this presentation may be the first time they are hearing your information.

The third common pitfall is that the presentation is **not targeted** to the audience's needs. When an informative presentation is off target, it may be because of the "look how smart I am" mindset. This is a common problem in informative presentations when the presenter's goal is to boost their own ego rather than meet the needs of their audience. Typically this is done subconsciously, but nevertheless it can hamstring your presentation from the get-go. In the next chapter, we'll go into more detail about the audience, but for now, remember that you need to be specific about the information you present and how it impacts your audience.

## PRESENTATIONS THAT PERSUADE

Persuasive presentations, like informational presentations, are extremely common in organizations. They get people to do things. They're all about making the sale, recruiting the help you need, or getting a commitment from someone to act. Persuasive presentations answer the question "Why?" Why should I buy this? Why should I support you? Or follow you? Or give you my discretionary effort?

Persuasion is often thought of as a skill associated with sales professionals, and it doesn't always have the most positive connotation. I like the way Jay Conger, professor of leadership studies at Claremont McKenna College, describes this powerful skill: "Persuasion is much more than a selling technique …

> "Effective persuasion is a learning and negotiating process for leading your colleagues to a shared solution to a problem."

It represents the opposite of deception. Effective persuasion is a learning and negotiating process for leading your colleagues to a shared solution to a problem." Persuasive presentations are much more than just sales pitches. They can be budget requests, new-product development pitches, job interviews, and advocacy for behavior change.

## MEET AMANDA

### *Amanda Salerno, Account Executive for Activate Consulting*

Amanda Salerno has been in the consulting business for the past five years. She loves helping clients solve problems and likes the fast pace of being on the front line of business development.

In her role as an account executive for Activate Consulting, Amanda has an opportunity to pitch her business's services to Singular Software, a major customer relationship management company. This is by far the largest opportunity she's been involved with, and her ability to get it across the finish line depends on how she does in the final proposal presentation to the leaders at Singular. If she is successful, it will change the trajectory of her career.

Amanda's presentation will be persuasive—she wants to persuade Singular to accept her proposal. If you've ever sold a product, pitched an idea, or raised funds for your favorite charity, you've engaged in persuasion. From running for president to interviewing for that dream job, persuasion is about convincing someone or some group about what they should think, feel, or do. It might just be the oldest communication skill in the world. After all, someone had to convince their tribal colleagues to go on the dangerous hunt before they could come back to the village to tell a story about it. Fortunately for Amanda, we'll provide her with the tools she needs to put together a great persuasive case.

## THE CHALLENGES WITH PERSUADING

Persuasive communication has power. In many situations, it can serve to bring better outcomes, but because it is so powerful, it also has the power to cause harm. Deceitful presenters, for example, can manipulate their audiences to their own ends by presenting incomplete facts and data. Socrates and Plato, great philosophers in the art of persuasion, were aware of these dangers. They warned of the Sophists—a school of teachers who valued winning more than the truth. Another way these devious presenters can influence their audiences is to disproportionately appeal to the emotion of the listener without backing up their claim with reason. Good persuasive arguments are grounded in logic and use emotion to make the arguments relatable.

Another pitfall of persuasive communication is alienating an audience that does not agree or is not convinced by your arguments, particularly in sales situations. I've seen presenters put their credibility and relationship with their client in jeopardy because they were unwilling to yield. There is a guideline in legal arguments called the rule of restraint. It states that you should use the narrowest set of propositions to prove a point and make strong arguments. Do not grasp at every possible but improbable proposition. I'd say that rule applies in business communication as well. In addition to making your best case, you also need to know when to stop arguing with your customers.

## PRESENTATIONS THAT INSPIRE

Inspirational presentations help people deal with change, move forward, or overcome an obstacle. To inspire is to fill someone with the urge or ability to do or feel something—and to be filled with creative energy. We're familiar with inspirational speeches from history, drama, and movies. In perhaps the most famous speech of the late twentieth century, Dr. Martin Luther King Jr. inspired the Civil Rights Movement by envisioning a world where people are judged by the content of their character and not the color of their skin. In the business world, inspirational presentations may seem less dramatic, but they are no less necessary in moving organizations forward.

If persuasive presentations convince the mind to come to a rational conclusion, inspirational presentations appeal to the heart. They draw on emotions—the desire to do our very best, the impulse to fight for what's right, or the strength to overcome an obstacle, to name a few. Leaders and managers set out on a mission, and it's part of their job to connect employees to that mission. In doing so, they equip them to take on tough challenges and to find the very best in themselves in difficult situations. The leader's voice resonates most clearly when it is inspiring us.

## MEET CHERYL
### *Cheryl Klein, Executive Director, Sales and Marketing, Tribune Products*

Tribune Products is a large consumer goods conglomerate. Cheryl Klein is the new vice president of sales and marketing for Tribune's household cleaning products—the company's second-largest division. While Tribune Products is a household name, several new companies boasting natural products have begun taking a huge market share. Tribune has made formulation changes and recently updated its household products' brand look and packaging. Sales, however, have been down, and the company's sales and marketing team is feeling frustrated and demoralized by Tribune's state in the marketplace. To add insult to injury, Tribune's competitors have been developing new products that are doing quite well in testing.

Cheryl is a seasoned sales and marketing professional. Tribune promoted Cheryl to this role with the expectation that her broad experience would help revitalize the sales and marketing team. While she will have many communication challenges ahead unique to being a leader of people,

> **The leader's voice resonates most clearly when it is inspiring us.**

her immediate communication situation is giving a presentation on the main stage at the upcoming company meeting. Her talk will include explaining and persuading, but she knows that her primary purpose is to inspire.

## THE CHALLENGES WITH INSPIRING

Inspirational presentations may be the most challenging type to give. Whether it's a small group like a team or a large group like the one Cheryl will speak to, inspirational presentations deal less with appeals to reason and logic and more to feelings, beliefs, and values. Speakers who aim to inspire need to convey a sense of **presence**, which in this context is about creating a bond among audience members based on a common value or belief. Another important task for speakers when giving inspirational talks is to resonate with the audience. **Resonance** in inspirational presentations is the ability to articulate the unexpressed feelings of the audience. When a speaker can do this, their message connects with the audience, and people are more likely to believe them.

For Cheryl, this means that she must tap into the frustration that members of her team feel about the current situation. After all, they're competitive sales and marketing professionals—they don't want to lose. Cheryl needs to employ and express empathy. She needs to share her own frustration without falling into a common trap of complaining or blaming. Her message will have a much better chance of resonating with her audience if she articulates the common sentiment of the audience. Then she can make her case for change. She'll need to help her listeners understand why this change is so important. She'll need to provide some direction on how to make the change. And finally, she can draw on shared values like competitiveness or commitment to the organization's mission to motivate them to go forward.

## OVERPLAYING EMOTION

Centuries ago, Aristotle devised a formula for effective rhetoric, or the art of making an effective persuasive speech. It included **ethos**, the speaker's credibility; **pathos**, the use of emotion; and **logos**, the use of argument and reasoning in making one's case. One of the dangers of inspirational presentations is that they can rely too heavily on pathos. They can become syrupy and melodramatic. When someone tugs too hard on our heartstrings, especially in business, we become a bit skeptical. All great presentations and speeches appeal to emotion—it is an essential element of persuasion. But if it's overplayed, emotion can work against you.

## MISSING THE MARK ON THE AUDIENCE

Audience analysis is a critical step in all presentation development, as we'll see in the next chapter. But missing the mark on the climate of the audience is courting disaster in an inspirational presentation. As we discussed, good presenters can resonate with the audience when they deliver inspirational presentations. But if you don't know them, how they are feeling, and what they are going through, you won't succeed. A great example of missing the mark with the audience was the town hall debate between former president George H. W. Bush and Bill Clinton in 1992. Not a business presentation, but a poignant example of not resonating with the audience.

During a town hall debate, the candidates were asked a question by a twenty-six-year-old woman named Marisa Hall: "How has the national debt personally affected each of your lives?" She continued, "And if it hasn't, how can you honestly find a cure for the economic problems of the common people if you have no experience in what's ailing them?"

President Bush, who had glanced at his watch while the question was being asked, answered first by saying, "Well, I think the national debt affects everybody." The questioner pressed on, asking about how it affected him personally. The president tried to elaborate by talking about parents affording an education for their children and added, "Are you suggesting that if somebody has means that the national debt doesn't affect them?"

The difficult interchange went on for a few more minutes as President Bush gave an impersonal and circuitous answer. It was clear from the audience that the president had missed the mark. He hadn't realized that what the questioner was seeking was empathy—a response that would have communicated, "You understand me" or "You care about me." His response did not resonate with her, and as we now know, it did not resonate with many viewers. Bush's poll numbers began to decline shortly after this debate.

## Chapter 3 Key Takeaways

- Informative presentations impart and explain new information. They're a staple of many business situations, but they run the risk of boring, overloading, or alienating the audience.
- Persuasive presentations convince the audience to think, feel, or do something in service of a larger goal. A logically sound

and emotionally appealing argument is powerful, but avoid manipulating audiences or overusing emotional appeals.

- Inspirational presentations motivate the audience to overcome an obstacle or improve themselves. They appeal to feelings, values, and motives—but if the presenter's message doesn't resonate with the audience, it will fall flat.

# CHAPTER 4
# Analyze Your Audience

When I get ready to talk to people, I spend two-thirds
of the time thinking (about) what they want to hear
and one-third thinking about what I want to say.

*—Abraham Lincoln*

Knowing your audience is the most foundational of all business communication skills. Why is that? In business, your audience wants to get something pragmatic from your presentation—new knowledge to do their job, evidence to help them make decisions, or inspiration to carry on in the face of adversity. Without knowing your audience, you can't address their primary concerns. Now that you're clear on the mission and objective of your presentation, let's explore the other component of the communication situation: the audience.

As a presenter, you must address the concerns of the audience. You may be a very charismatic speaker, but if your job is to update the executive team on a critical project and you don't provide accurate and easily digestible information, you've failed at your chief responsibility. As presenters, we must know our audience to address their needs. That doesn't mean we should pander or expect everyone in the audience to agree with (or even like) what we have to say. But as professionals, we are expected to understand who they are and why they are there.

## Analyze Your Audience

Where do we start, then? Well, first you've got to start asking questions and getting curious about your audience. We've developed a set of six questions that you can ask to get a better sense of how to shape elements of your presentation to fit the needs and desires of your audience.

### QUESTION 1—WHO ARE THEY?

Knowing the demographics of your audience is important. You may be familiar with the individuals in your own organization, but it would still behoove you to have a good understanding of who's going to be in the room for your presentation. If you are presenting for prospects that you don't know too well or giving a presentation at a conference or event, getting even basic demographic information will help you shape your presentation and the content it contains. A simple example of this would be the average age of your audience members.

> **As presenters, we must know our audience to address their needs.**

Referring to a television show from the 1980s when presenting to millennials would be about as effective as using a TikTok video in a presentation for a room full of baby boomers.

In addition to basic demographics, a person's role within an organization plays a key part in how they receive information. It should impact how you present that information to them as well. Presenting to the senior team, for instance, is different than presenting to a class of new hires. Both groups need specific kinds of information that are packaged and framed in ways that meet their needs. You're almost guaranteed to get less time with the senior team, and the decisions they make are drastically different than those of a new hire. But sometimes it's not always this clear cut, so here are some questions to ask when seeking to understand the demographics and roles that members of your audience play:

- What are the basic demographics of the audience: geography, age, gender?
- What are their job titles?
- What kinds of decisions are they making?
- What degree of influence do they have in the organization?
- How long have they been in their role?
- Who do they report to in the organization?

## QUESTION 2—WHY ARE THEY HERE?

The question "Why are they here?" helps you get at the motivation of your audience. Knowing this will help you craft your message to be as influential as possible. Start by understanding why members of your audience are attending your presentation and what they'll do with your message. Are they decision makers for this organization? Will they evaluate your message and report it to someone else? Will they make a recommendation based on what you say? Understanding why someone is listening to you will make a difference in what you say in your messaging.

Maybe your audience is there because they've been told to be there by their managers. In my career, I have led many training sessions where people were required to attend. If you're going into a presentation where people don't believe they need to be there or would rather be somewhere else, you should start out with a clear, concise statement of what's in it for them. On the other hand, if you have an audience that is anxiously awaiting your findings or your point of view on a topic, you can unfold that information in an intriguing way that builds suspense, like Steve Jobs would do at Apple events. These are subtle but significant changes in how you approach a presentation, but they pay big dividends in how the audience responds to you.

## QUESTION 3—WHAT DO THEY KNOW?

How much prior knowledge an audience has about your presentation will change the amount of time you spend on background and explanation. It will also help determine how technical and detailed your presentation needs to be. You wouldn't present the results of a medical study to a group of doctors the same way you would to a group of sales professionals. These two groups of professionals have different levels of domain knowledge. Here are some questions to consider when mining for what your audience knows:

- How much knowledge do they have about your subject matter?
- How much detail do they need to understand your topic?
- What historical information do they need to understand your topic?
- What specialized language should you avoid given the audience's current knowledge?

## QUESTION 4—WHAT DO THEY WANT?

What drives your audience? Understanding what's in it for them may be the most important aspect of audience analysis. If you don't understand what matters most to your audience, you'll never be successful in positioning your message in a way that resonates with them. Great presenters make connections between what they want to accomplish and what an audience wants by finding common ground where both presenter and audience are on the same footing.

For instance, if I'm presenting an idea on how to gain a competitive advantage using a new but risky technology to an audience of risk-averse decision makers, I know I need to frame my message in a way that promotes the risk management aspect of my plan. If I knew my audience valued bold action and was more concerned with the differentiation they could achieve with my solution, I would frame my presentation to emphasize the competitive advantage of the new technology.

> **Understanding what's in it for them may be the most important aspect of audience analysis.**

This doesn't mean I wouldn't talk about the risk, but I'd focus more of my effort on what I know my audience values. Here are some questions to consider about your audience's drive:

- What are their core concerns? How do they balance their financial, organizational, and psychological concerns in their business?
- Why are they coming to your presentation?
- What current problems are affecting them?

## QUESTION 5—WHAT DO THEY BELIEVE?

Thinking about the beliefs or the attitude that your audience has about your topic allows you to understand whether they are predisposed to immediately agree or disagree with you. This will help you know whether or not you need to do extra convincing. A person presenting on the efficacy of a vaccine would present differently to a group that believes in the safety of modern vaccines than to a group that does not. Here are some questions to consider about your audience's beliefs:

- What cultural considerations should you think about?
- To what degree do they agree with your point of view?
- Why might they resist your message?

## QUESTION 6—DO THEY TRUST YOU?

Your audience will never take anything you say to heart if they don't find you credible. A presenter who has never worked in academia might have to overcome audience skepticism if they are pitching a solution to a university board of regents. Understanding how your background influences your audience's experience of you is key to getting buy-in for your presentation. Here are some questions to consider when determining how much your audience trusts you:

- What do they know about you, your company, and your product or message?
- Does your audience believe you are a credible authority on this information?

# How to Gather Information about Your Audience

Depending on the situation, gathering information to answer these questions may be as simple as drawing on what you already know from everyday experience. In other instances where you know the audience less, you may need to conduct formal interviews to gain a deeper insight into the people to whom you're presenting. You can use information found in your company directory, in annual reports, on LinkedIn, or on other social media platforms. You can ask colleagues who have worked with the people who will be in your audience. You can—and should—reach out to people prior to your presentation to learn more about their roles, their level of knowledge, and what they're looking for from your presentation.

## How Your Audience Sees You

As we touched on with our questions related to trust, knowing your audience is not just about what you know about them but about what they know or don't know about you. All that knowledge helps the audience shape their perception of you. You'll want to do whatever you can to make this as positive an image as possible. **Ethos**, or speaker credibility, is a very important aspect of public communication. Successful presenters understand how to manage their ethos. We will explore this from two perspectives in this book. While we're discussing planning and developing our presentation, we'll address the importance of what you build into your presentation to help you establish credibility. Later in the book, we'll look at how you establish trust when you deliver the presentation.

Here's a grid with the key audience information for each of our characters. After you review, complete these questions for your presentation. For making your presentation, you can find the audience analysis at www.talentisvital.com.

# Character Analysis Grid

|  | CHUCK | AMANDA | CHERYL |
|---|---|---|---|
| **WHO ARE THEY?** | Decision makers and leaders of the company | Key decision makers Users of the service | Colleagues |
| **WHY ARE THEY HERE?** | They want to know if there are any concerns with the project and plans for mitigation | To confirm their under-standing of the offering To make a go/no-go decision | To find out more about their future |
| **WHAT DO THEY KNOW?** | Strong under-standing of context with varying degrees of detailed project knowledge | Moderate understanding of the Activate process | They are losing in the market They don't know much about the new products in development |
| **WHAT DO THEY WANT?** | Information to help make decisions | A creative approach A level of comfort in the partner | Assurances Concrete information |

| | | | |
|---|---|---|---|
| **WHAT DO THEY BELIEVE?** | Business considerations may require changes in strategy | This is a big decision that could have significant ramifications if the partnership is not successful | They are distrustful |
| **DO THEY TRUST YOU?** | Chuck is still establishing his level of credibility and trust with this audience. | Amanda has established rapport and a level of trust, but she is still earlier in her career, and the client may still have some concerns about her experience | They trust Cheryl but not the company. |

# Selecting Your Specific Objective

Now that you have a good understanding of your audience, it's time to develop a specific objective. In all communication, **you must be clear on the specific objective of your message**—What do you want to happen because of what you say? When you have a specific objective, you can develop a tight presentation and avoid irrelevant or distracting information. A simple technique for bringing this into focus is to think about what you want your audience to know, feel, or do at the end of your presentation. I call this the Know-Feel-Do Matrix.

## THE KNOW-FEEL-DO MATRIX

We use a simple gridded chart—or matrix—to visualize the audience's perspective based on what they know, what they feel, and what they do. We also want to show the movement of the audience from where they are prior to the presentation to where you would like them to be after you've presented. By working through the Know-Feel-Do Matrix, you'll become laser focused on your objectives. As an example, I've also provided what the Know-Feel-Do Matrix looks like for our various characters. Here's what it looks like:

## Know-Feel-Do Matrix

|      | FROM | TO |
|------|------|-----|
| KNOW |      |     |
| FEEL |      |     |
| DO   |      |     |

## The Know-Feel-Do Matrix for Chuck

|      | FROM | TO |
|------|------|-----|
| KNOW | Uncertain about the status of the study<br>Unsure about whether or not they will meet the important project timelines<br>Unclear about what needs to be done to complete the project on time | Understand exactly where they are in the study timeline<br>Understand the risks associated with meeting the timeline and how those risks will be mitigated<br>Know what decisions they need to make and the implications of those decisions |
| FEEL | Worried about the risks associated with the project<br>Uncertain of the implications a delay may have on other organizational functions | Assured that Chuck and his team can manage the project risks<br>Informed about all the ramifications of the project risks |
| DO   | Withholding additional resources<br>Debating whether to move forward with this project | Continue to support the project and provide needed resources |

# The Know-Feel-Do Matrix for Amanda

|  | FROM | TO |
|---|---|---|
| **KNOW** | Unclear on the specifics of how Activate's team will engage with the in-house marketing team | Clear on Activate's engagement model and how they can move quickly to integrate the teams |
| **FEEL** | Worried about the risks associated with committing to Activate as a partner | Secure in their decision to go with Activate |
| **DO** | Hiring contract employees to fill the gaps in marketing | Hiring Activate to manage and deliver key marketing projects |

# The Know-Feel-Do Matrix for Cheryl

|  | FROM | TO |
|---|---|---|
| **KNOW** | Uncertain about the future of the company<br>Do not understand the reasons for such large staff reductions | Grasp how the company plans to return to a leadership position in the industry<br>Comprehend the decision rationale for staff reductions |
| **FEEL** | Worried about their own future and that of their families<br>Concerned for their friends who lost their jobs | Energized about their future with the company and the prospects for success<br>Reassured that the company has acted responsibly in separating employees |
| **DO** | Frozen and not engaging in work or the change effort | Recommitted to the company and to fully join in serving customers and helping the company regain its prominence |

Earlier you'll recall we discussed the idea of dialing in the right amount of explaining, persuading, and inspiring in your presentations. You'll need to do some of each in almost every presentation you give. Completing the Know-Feel-Do Matrix will help you understand your audience's perspective and how you can dial in the right kind of presentation for your audience. By looking at this shift, you can craft an achievable objective that will guide you in developing the rest of your presentation.

## Chapter 4 Key Takeaways

- Establish your credibility (or ethos) before your presentation by reading published material on your audience, interviewing them to gauge their goals and expectations, and interviewing people who have worked with them.

- There are six key questions you must answer during audience analysis:

  □ **Who are they?** What is your audience's demographic information? What role do they play in the company? What decisions are they making?

  □ **Why are they here?** What is the audience's motivation for attending your presentation? Will they make a decision based on your presentation? Will they report your information to someone else? Were they required to attend?

  □ **What do they know?** What prior knowledge do they have of your topic? What knowledge or jargon will you need to explain, elaborate on, or avoid?

  □ **What do they want?** What current problems is your audience trying to solve? What drives them as a discourse community (financially, psychologically, organizationally)?

  □ **What do they believe?** What are your audience's personal, organizational, and cultural values? How much will they agree with or resist your message?

    ◻ **Do they trust you?** Does your audience know you and your message, or will you have to establish your credibility?

- Use the Know-Feel-Do Matrix to visualize movement of the audience from where they are prior to the presentation (regarding what they know, feel, or do) to where you would like them to be after you've presented.

CHAPTER 5

# Develop Your Ideas

There is one thing stronger than all the armies in the world, and that is an idea whose time has come.

—*Victor Hugo*

By conducting an analysis of your audience's needs, beliefs, and perspectives, you gain a deeper understanding of the people to whom you are presenting. By using the Know-Feel-Do Matrix, you clarify where they fall today and where you want them to be after your presentation. The final element of responding to the communication situation is to combine everything we've done thus far and develop the ideas you want to present. This means you'll need to think through the issues associated with your topic. These issues will form the basis of your presentation content. Essentially, these ideas are what you'll be talking about to your audience.

## Develop Your Ideas

### CAN YOU ARTICULATE YOUR MAIN IDEA?

Let's start with a clear and succinct statement of the main idea. The main idea, sometimes called the through line or the big idea, will serve as a backbone for your entire presentation. All your content decisions from this point on will be in service of supporting, illustrating, or deepening your audience's understanding of your main idea. The good news is that your main idea will flow naturally from the preparation you've already done. You've looked at the communication situation, you've completed the Know-Feel-Do Matrix, and you've examined your audience. To develop the statement of your main idea, put these elements together to express your firm point of view. A good statement of the main idea should include a "what" and a "why." It should answer the question, "What is the most important thing I want my audience to remember, and why is it important to them?"

To dive deeper into the concept of the main idea, let's look at what Amanda has come up with. Based on her preparation, she decides that the main idea of her presentation is "**Activate's unique engagement process will accelerate your marketing campaigns and reduce long-term marketing costs.**" It includes the what—"Activate's unique engagement process"—and the why—"it accelerates marketing campaigns and reduces cost." Her audience may not restate it the same way, but Amanda will want them to be able to remember and repeat the following idea: "Activate's approach is different and will help us get the results we need at the right price." Everything in her presentation should support and illustrate this main idea.

> A good statement of the main idea should include a "what" and a "why." It should answer the question, "What is the most important thing I want my audience to remember, and why is it important to them?"

After all, if her audience believes that Activate can get things done and save them money, why wouldn't they select them as their vendor?

What did Amanda do to arrive at the main idea of her presentation? She looked at the communication situation, her objective, the Know-Feel-Do Matrix, and the audience. After considering all this information, she crafted a single sentence that communicates her point of view.

> **To develop your supporting ideas, you'll need to look at your main idea and think about ways to explain, explore, support, or expand on it.**

Next, Amanda will need to identify the important issues that are associated with, and support, her main idea. These are the claims that arise from this main idea that must be explained or defended. Here are some examples: What is the proven engagement process? How will working with Activate accelerate marketing campaigns? How will working with Activate save costs? How much will it save? In classical rhetoric, this process is known as invention. Invention is an organized way of discovering the content of the communication, whether it's a speech, letter, or in our case, a presentation.

## FIND YOUR SUPPORTING IDEAS

To develop your supporting ideas, you'll need to look at your main idea and think about ways to explain, explore, support, or expand on it. This process requires some inquisitive thinking. Two methods can be of great help in exploring the topics and ideas that could be included in the presentation. One is a very structured left-brain activity while the other is a more free-flowing right-brain activity. I suggest experimenting with both. One may suit you better based on your personality or work style, or you may find one to be more effective for presentations with different purposes. The first method is called **the journalist's grid**. Here's how to do it: Make a table with two columns. In the left-hand column, develop questions the way a journalist would: Who? What? Where? When? Why? How? In the right-hand column, write the answer and describe why it matters. These answers will form the foundation of your presentation. Here's how Amanda might use it:

| JOURNALIST'S QUESTION | YOUR ANSWER AND WHY IT MATTERS |
|---|---|
| Who will be leading this project? | Our team of experienced consultants. All of our consultants have over ten years of relevant experience working with software firms like yours. You get the benefit of our expertise. |
| What is your "unique" approach? | Based on our experience, we've combined a set of custom-developed tools and templates that quickly capture stakeholder input, reduce rework, and simplify the review process. |
| Where have you done this before? | Our team has worked on major marketing initiatives with Fortune 50 software and tech firms in fifteen countries, including [insert examples]. You can be assured that we have the experience to handle a large-scale, high-profile project like this. |
| When can we expect results? | Projects like yours typically begin to yield results ninety days after implementation. The reason for this is [insert reasons]. |
| Why are you able to reduce long-term costs? | Our market target method allows us to reach more qualified prospects, so you spend less to find the leads you're looking for. |
| How do you structure your contracts? | Our contracts are structured on a time-and-materials basis. This allows you to closely manage the project fees. |

The second approach is called **mind mapping**. This is a brain-storming method that helps you identify the relevant topics that might be included in your presentation. First, write your main idea in the center of a sheet of paper, and draw a circle around it. Next, draw lines out from the circle with words or brief phrases that will be important in communicating the idea. Once you've completed that first round, expand those supporting points to include subtopics, relevant facts, statistics, arguments, and other information. Continue expanding your mind map until you have several layers of detail. This will give you an idea of the content you should include in your presentation. Here's a look at what Amanda's mind map might look like:

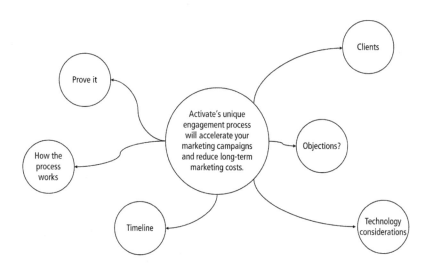

# Chapter 5 Key Takeaways

- The main idea is your presentation's central claim, usually contained in a one-sentence thesis statement. It is the essence of your message.
- Key takeaways are important points that you want to make sure your audience remembers or clearly understands by the time they leave. These takeaways should support your main idea.

# CHAPTER 6

# Structure Your Presentation

If you confuse them, you lose them.

—*Anonymous*

Once you've identified your main and supporting ideas, it's time to organize them into a logical and digestible message. Here you will make important decisions about what content to include or eliminate and how to structure your message.

We've probably all sat through a presentation and when it was over asked, "What was the point?" Maybe it left you feeling confused or unsure about what you were supposed to do with the information you received. In some cases, you may have even wondered whether the presenter was clear on what they were trying to communicate. In those situations, it's immediately apparent that the presenter hadn't done the important work of organizing their ideas in a logical fashion. In this section, we're going to look at two concepts to help organize the ideas in your presentation so that your audience understands your message clearly: structure and patterns.

**Structure** is the overarching form of the presentation. A **pattern** is the way you put your content elements together. As Barbara Minto, author of the *Pyramid Principle*, says, "Controlling the sequence of information and ideas is at the heart of clarity." In classical rhetoric, developing the structures and patterns in a speech is called arrangement. Of all the places a presentation could go wrong, the most damaging is a lack of structure. That's because, as we know from adult learning theory, audiences like structure. They like to know where they're going and how you intend to get them there. If you confuse them, you lose them.

In many ways, a good presentation is like a three-act play. Good presentations have three major sections: a beginning, a middle, and an end. Each of these sections can be divided into subsections that include important details—like how acts are made up of individual scenes. All of these sections are linked together with transitions. Transitions help the audience follow your thinking. This three-section structure—beginning, middle, and end—is as ancient as Aeschylus, the father of Greek tragedy. And it still works! But the way you use each of these elements can make the difference between crickets and a standing ovation at the end of your presentation. In presentations, we also call these three parts the opening, the body, and the conclusion.

## The Opening

In a good story, the opening sets the stage, introduces the main characters, and presents a problem or challenge the hero must overcome. A classic example is the Academy Award–winning thriller *Jaws*. In the opening, we learn that the story takes place in a beach town during summer. Lots of tourists will be visiting the beach, all looking forward to relaxing and having fun. Suddenly, a dangerous shark attacks several swimmers, and panic overtakes the townspeople and visitors. How will the vacationers be safe from danger? That is the problem the story's hero, Chief Brody, must solve. The opening of *Jaws* draws the audience in and makes them want to see what happens. For Chuck, his opening sets up the following question: Where is our drug along the development timeline, and will it finish on time?

The opening of your presentation should serve a similar purpose: it should provide the necessary background and context while also presenting the problem or idea the presentation hopes to address or resolve. Later, we'll help you craft the perfect introduction so that the beginning of your presentation hooks the audience the way a good story does.

## The Body

The body is the heart of your presentation. It's where you will lay out the most crucial information. It's where you make your case, present your evidence, and offer the supporting data and examples your audience needs in order to act. Here is where you incorporate the organizing patterns we'll discuss in a moment.

## The Conclusion

The conclusion of your presentation is where you summarize your key points, make your ask, and leave your audience with a powerful mental image or idea that will serve as a vivid reminder of your message.

## Transitions

Transitions are the way you help your audience follow your reasoning. They're like the synapses in our nervous system that allow one neuron to pass a chemical or electrical signal to another neuron. Transitions keep the story flowing.

## The Importance of Organization

Why so much emphasis on organizing information? Because it helps the audience follow the story and see the logic in your thinking. Good structure makes complex ideas easier to digest and remember. To demonstrate, here's a little activity that we run in our workshop to highlight how important it is for information to be well organized. I tell participants that I'm going to show them a series of symbols and give them fifteen seconds to remember them in order. Then I show them this:

> ## Good structure makes complex ideas easier to digest and remember.

!@#$%#%@!$$#%@!@%!$##@%$!

When their time is up, I ask them if anyone can remember all twenty-five symbols in the correct order. No one ever raises their hand. So far, I haven't encountered anyone with a photographic memory willing to put it to the test in front of their peers. Then, after we have a few laughs, I ask them to memorize this pattern instead:

!!!!!@@@@@#####$$$$$%%%%%

And an "Aha!" echoes through the classroom. It's a eureka moment. Suddenly, the value of structure and patterns becomes clear. This is a classic example of information entropy. It's a scientific term that refers to the amount of disorder or randomness in a system. The first set of icons had a high level of information entropy because the symbols were arranged randomly. You couldn't predict what would come next. The second set of icons were grouped together by symbol, which made it much easier to remember. Our brains are pattern seekers. As listeners, we want low information entropy. We want order. It's hard to work with chaos.

Structure and patterns help make your message memorable. If it's not, your audience won't be able to act on it later. And in today's world, where we are constantly consuming and conveying information, getting people to remember information is challenging at best. The **Ebbinghaus Forgetting Curve** shows that within an hour, audience members forget an average of 50 percent of information in a presentation. Within twenty-four hours, they'll lose about 70 percent of the information you delivered. Within a week, they'll fail to recollect up to 90 percent of your presentation. You need to beat that curve if you want your presentation to be a success.

## Pick a Pattern

Earlier, you identified the important ideas to include in your presentation. Now you need to arrange them for maximum impact. Hidden behind most business presentations is a pattern that gives the presentation a clarity boost. Let's look at three common patterns that can help you organize your material so that it's easy for your audience to follow. Then we'll look at how each of our characters can use one of the patterns to help them achieve their communication objective. There are many patterns to choose from, so we've made them available to you on our website (www.talentisvital.com).

The three patterns we'll explore are the report pattern, the problem-solution pattern, and the elimination-order pattern. The **report pattern** is great when you need to share information with your audience. It's the pattern most closely connected to what you want your audience to know when using the Know-Feel-Do Matrix. With the report pattern, you'll be presenting a lot of data, but data is dry and boring. You've got to make the data come to life by converting the information you've gathered into insights that further the audience's understanding of a situation. The report pattern organizes information by answering the questions "What? Why? Who? Where? When? How?" *Back of the Napkin* author Dan Roam refers to it as six-mode thinking and posits that it is a cognition model that can break down any problem, idea, or story into six different modes of information. If you used the journalist's grid to develop your presentation content, you have everything you need to use the report pattern.

A good informative or explanatory presentation generally starts with "What?" because it provides context: "What are we doing here?" Then, once the scene is set, it answers the "Why?" question: "Why are we listening to you?" Adults need to know that up front, or you'll lose them quickly. After you've provided your reasons, the next question to address would be "How?" ("How are we going to do it?"). These should then be followed by some combination of "Who?" ("Who's doing the work?"), "When?" ("When does it need to be done by?"), and "Where?" ("Where will all this happen?"). The beauty of the report pattern is that it's good for describing just about anything past or future. For example, what did we do? Or what will we do? Why did we do it? Or why should we do it?

You might recognize the **elimination-order pattern** from your favorite courtroom drama. It's the last ten minutes of the episode when the defense is giving their closing arguments. They go through each of the prosecution's arguments and disprove them to the jury, proving their client's innocence. If you want to really prove your point, the elimination-order pattern describes other plausible solutions to a problem and then demonstrates why these are unworkable. What's left at the end is your solution—the only viable option forward. This pattern is very successful in persuading audiences. In fact, it's how many lawyers and scholars present their cases or studies.

In the book *They Say, I Say*, authors Gerald Graff and Cathy Birkenstein discuss the importance of entering a conversation using what the other person says (or thinks but doesn't say) as the launch pad for your own ideas. A persuasive presentation is based in argument, and to argue well, you need to do more than merely assert your own ideas. You need to respond to the other party's concerns. You're either for or against something that someone already believes, so make sure you know what's going on in your audience's head.

To illustrate this pattern, let's check in with Amanda and her presentation to Singular Software. Prior to making her final sales presentation, Amanda uncovered Singular's major concerns about engaging a large consultancy to lead their new marketing campaign. Amanda can use the elimination-order pattern to demonstrate how her proposal addresses each of these concerns. After an attention-grabbing opening, she can list each concern and describe how Activate has addressed similar client concerns in the past, providing vivid examples and case studies for each.

A close cousin to the elimination-order pattern is the **problem-solution pattern**. This is a very common pattern used in persuasive business presentations. It's pragmatic and easy to follow. As the name implies, you describe a problem, analyze the causes, and provide a solution. With the problem-solution pattern, you can easily combine emotion and logic—two elements of Aristotle's formula for persuasion. When using this pattern, you describe the problem and add the emotional element by conveying the impact of the problem. In her presentation, Cheryl introduces the problem of declining sales; it's easy to see the downturn by looking at a simple chart. But what's the impact on the audience?

Cheryl can help her audience internalize the problem by describing the ramifications of shrinking sales. Declining sales can affect everything from the brand's position in the market to a reduction in workforce. At a bare minimum, her audience understands that lower sales numbers signal that a change is needed. That is the hard reality of business. In her presentation, Cheryl must convey a sense of urgency. This is emotional. The company is on the burning platform—they're experiencing the moment when the necessity of change outweighs the fear of unknown consequences. This metaphor comes from the inner struggle of an oil rig worker who must decide whether to stay on the rig that just caught fire or risk jumping into a sea of burning oil. Cheryl must impart to her audience that her company's declining sales must compel everyone to action or they all risk going down in a fiery blaze.

Once Cheryl states the problem and its severity, she can detail her solution, revealing how it will alleviate the discomfort of the current situation. She can introduce her plan to realign the sales team, rebrand the products, and adjust the incentive compensation plan— all concrete actions that will lead to success. This is the clarity that her audience desires. They want to know how she will lead the company to success. They want to feel secure in their commitment. And they want to know what their role is in the future of the company. The problem-solution pattern is the perfect way for Cheryl to address her audience and inspire them to act.

Finally, here's a bonus pattern that was first introduced to me by a colleague of mine. Several years ago, I attended a client meeting to help facilitate some organizational changes. The business unit vice president asked each of her direct reports to prepare a presentation with their perceptions of the issues and challenges facing the organization. She allotted thirty minutes for each speaker. As she invited the final person up to present, she got an urgent call from her boss regarding a customer issue that needed to be resolved immediately. After she put down the phone, she looked to the final presenter and said, "Paul, you've got five minutes."

To his credit, Paul was prepared and was able to condense his half-hour talk to just the key messages. He distilled the essence of his main idea using my favorite pattern of all: **What? So what? Now what?** In his presentation, Paul laid out the issue, demonstrated why it mattered, and outlined what he thought the company should do about it. This pattern succinctly and efficiently highlights your main idea, how it impacts your audience, and what needs to be done. Even if you never find yourself in Paul's situation, you should be able to give the What? So what? Now what? version of your presentation at any time. Taking the time to organize your ideas is a gift to your audience because it will increase their ability to follow you and understand you.

## Chapter 6 Key Takeaways

- Organize your information! The less information entropy your presentation structure has, the easier it will be for your audience to retain it.
- Early in your presentation, introduce the structure and pattern you will use. You don't need to bang them over the head with it, but let them know where you're going.
- Presentation patterns organize the body of your presentation into a digestible structure. There are many kinds, and some are more suited than others for each presentation purpose.
- Patterns that inform make information concrete and predictable.

- Patterns that persuade frame information in a way that demonstrates your point of view.
- Patterns that inspire contextualize challenging situations to motivate audience members.

CHAPTER 7

# Getting Your Ideas onto Slides with HINT

Packaging can be theater; it can create a story.

*—Steve Jobs*

## Create Message Packages with the HINT Method

The next step in the presentation development process is taking the ideas and research you've outlined and putting them into a linear slide presentation. If you remember from the first chapter, one of the distinguishing aspects of a presentation is that it uses dual-channel learning and therefore requires robust visual language. To take advantage of that aspect of presentations, we need to lay out the presentation—idea by idea, slide by slide—and incorporate the visual communication. This process is called **storyboarding**. Storyboarding is a technique used by film and television directors, and it refers to the shot-by-shot visual and scripted depiction of the story. As presentation developers, we're doing the same thing—creating the idea-by-idea, slide-based view of our presentation. Essentially, it's what each of your "shots" looks like. It's the **flow** of the story, which needs to go in order from start to finish.

You can think of this like the way a writer builds a story using paragraphs. But because a presentation is a visual form of communication, you won't be working with paragraphs as you would in a written communication. You'll be working with message packages. What is a message package? Let me give you a HINT. A **message package** is a unit that consists of an argument, an idea, or an assertion. These come in the form of a **headline** that states a key point or insight, an **image** to help visualize your message, **notes** that contain the accompanying support, such as reasons, facts, evidence, and examples, and a **transition** statement, the logical connection to the next slide. You build your presentation with a series of message packages that get your audience to the goal you set out in the Know-Feel-Do Matrix. It's everything you need to tell your story—one slide at a time. HINT is an acronym that will help you remember how to build a message package.

## Using HINT with Index Cards

When we work on this in our training programs, we use index cards to represent each slide, one card per slide. Sticky notes are good, too, but I find that presentation development takes me more than one session. Dealing with the ... well ... stickiness of sticky notes can be a distraction over multiple sessions. Index cards, on the other hand, offer several other benefits. You can use both sides easily. You can move them around on your desk and see the flow come to life. You can use different-colored cards for the major sections: opening, body, conclusion, and transitions. You can punch a hole in the upper left-hand corner, loop a rubber band through it, and have your flow available for rehearsal.

Of course, you can do all this in PowerPoint or Keynote—their slide-sorter mode acts like a storyboard. I recommend, however, that you start with cards and a pencil to avoid the temptation of using just bullet points or too many words. The index cards and your pencil help you think visually. The point of storyboarding is not to create perfectly polished slides. **The point is to blend the logic, language, and look** of your presentation. Depending on your personal preference, your storyboard can range from scribbling stick people on the index cards with a pencil, to using a set of colored pens, to sketching formal drawings.

## Strong Headlines Capture Each Slide's Main Idea

Your headline should summarize the main message of the slide. Good presentation headlines make a claim or unveil an insight, which is different from stating a topic. Unfortunately, many presenters get caught up in the familiar slideware template format of headline and body-text bullet points. And because the template headline font size is typically a whopping forty-four points, presenters feel constrained by the size and write headlines that are topic based—"Quarterly Sales" or "Our Mission," for example. These are headlines that introduce a topic. And the result of thinking in a topic mode is a data dump. Then they put all the information pertaining to the company mission or the quarterly sales results on the slide, and it becomes unclear what's most important.

When using the HINT method, I suggest you initially write the headline as a complete and concise sentence. It doesn't mean you'll necessarily use the full sentence or put the headline at the top of the slide. (I'll talk about text as a visual shortly.) It's a means of making your main idea, argument, or assertion clear to the audience. Here's an example: "Household Debt" is a topic-based headline. It tells us nothing important and is rife for a data dump full of mortgage statistics. Snooze! Compare that with "Household debt reaches its highest level in two years." This headline gives the audience much more information using just a few extra words.

Here's another example: If you are presenting your company's sales results, instead of a headline that reads, "Current Quarter Sales," create a headline that tells the audience something meaningful about the current quarter sales. Did they go up or down? Did they meet or exceed expectations? Was there some unique driver of the sales results? A better slide headline would be "Quarterly sales surpassed goal by 6 percent on strong final month." Now we know (and have a better chance of remembering) that sales results were good—above goal—and driven by something that happened in the third month of the quarter.

## MAKE YOUR HEADLINES "ACTION ORIENTED"

Business audiences are pragmatic. They want to know immediately what they can do with the information or ideas you're discussing. That's why you should give them a "Now what?" in the headline. This simple method helps you get right to the important information about a topic: "Demand for our product is growing. We need to expand capacity." This headline packs a lot of information into these two sentences. We learn that demand is growing, and the presenter thinks expanding capacity is necessary. You could make the headline more concise by saying, "Demand is growing—expansion is needed." Of course, you need to support those claims with facts, evidence, and reasons, but the main point is clear and unequivocal. Again, notice we are using a complete sentence.

Research supports this full-sentence approach. Michael Alley, author of *The Craft of Scientific Presentations: Critical Steps to Succeed and Critical Errors to Avoid* (Springer, 2005), conducted a study using two PowerPoint presentations, each with a different headline format. One presentation included only sentence fragments at the top of each slide. The second presentation included a complete sentence at the top that summarized the most important point of the slide. In tests to measure the knowledge and comprehension of the information in the presentations, the audiences who experienced the slides with the complete-sentence headlines saw an average improvement in test scores of eleven percentage points over the audiences who saw the slides with the sentence fragments.

When you use the slide headline to summarize your point for your audience members, you properly guide their attention, and in the process, you ease the burden on their working memory.

## Adding an Image

The idea here is to add your visual communication elements so you can fully develop your slides later in the process. Here you're sketching the visual story. It doesn't need to be fancy. It can be a simple sketch, but it needs to represent the visual that will be on the slide. This takes some thought. It's the step that some presenters often skip because they don't want to do the work necessary to conjure an image that helps communicate the message. So, they just throw the words on the screen, and usually they use too many. Remember, we said that one of the distinguishing characteristics of a good presentation is the robust incorporation of visual communication. Don't forget that a presentation is a multichannel learning experience—a place where audiences learn from both words and pictures. Richard E. Mayer, renowned educational psychologist, puts it simply: "People can learn more deeply from words and pictures than from words alone."

But you may worry that you're not a graphic designer. I understand. I'm not either. You don't need to be a graphic designer to add meaningful visuals. But good visual communication starts with having a concept. Here are a few tips for developing visual communication concepts. If you are answering a "What?" question, draw an object. For your "Who?" questions, show people. For the "When?" questions, put down a timeline. For "Where?" questions, provide a map. For questions that answer "How are they related?" include a chart. For the "How?" questions, make a process illustration. And for the "Why?" questions, show connections in an overview. For now, use simple shapes, lines, and curves (you know, stick figures!) to draft the visual elements. We'll go deeper into how to get better at designing the actual visual that will appear on the slide, but for now, decide what kind of visual you need. For now, just get your initial idea on paper or your index card.

> **Keep them simple and related to the message.**

The visual aspect of communication is easy to get wrong. Poorly conceived visuals can detract from the core message and can even be misleading. To make sure your visuals add to your presentation rather than detract, keep them simple and related to the message.

## Create Your Notes

If you want your audience to understand you, believe you, learn from you, buy from you, or be inspired by you, you need to support your arguments and assertions with proof and evidence. Your notes are where you put the illustration and examples you'll talk about.

Types of evidence to consider for your "N" section include quotes, examples, statistics, research findings, expert testimony, interviews, analogies, and data from surveys or studies. In chapter 9, we'll explore in more detail how to write the notes on the back of each index card.

# Plan Your Transitions

Transitions help you make the logical connections between ideas and slides visible to the audience. How often have you sat through a presentation and lost focus? Maybe you catch yourself drifting, or you're just not sure where the presenter is going. Part of the reason poor presenters lose their audiences is that they fail to keep things directed toward a final goal. They have too many out-of-place twists and turns. Sometimes these distractions are caused by a lack of structural planning when building the presentation. Other times, they result from a lack of discipline in delivery, such as when a speaker goes on an unrelated tangent. Regardless of the cause, the effect is the same: the audience is confused.

Earlier we established that listeners seek order and structure. As presenters, we want to give them a low information entropy environment—not too much chaos. We must make it easy for the listener to follow us. Any mental energy spent trying to make sense of a disjointed presentation is energy not available for considering the substantive issues of your presentation. The way to help the listener stay with you as you move through your presentation is to incorporate well-thought-out transitions.

Transitions are like street signs. In fact, they are often called signposts. They tell the audience where you are now and where you're going next. Generally, they consist of a short statement about what just happened and then an orientation to what will be coming next. Here are some common examples:

- "We've talked about x; let's move on to y."
- "We've learned x, but what does this have to do with y?"
- "We now understand x, but let's see what ramifications this has for y."

One way to think of transitions would be to compare them to neural synapses. Every minute of every day, your brain is constantly sending signals out to your whole body. This is how we feel heat, cold, a lover's touch, the smell of dinner, or the myriad senses we experience every day. For a nerve impulse to continue to move through the nervous system, it must "transition" or jump via a synapse. The synapse transitions the impulse from one nerve to another. That's what needs to happen in a presentation. You must set up transmitters to keep the presentation moving.

## Example: Building Out Your Deck with HINT

Let's look at an example with Cheryl. Her presentation purpose is to inspire, but her dials include some informing and some persuading. Here's a reminder of her Know-Feel-Do Matrix.

|  | FROM | TO |
|---|---|---|
| **KNOW** | Uncertain about the future of the company<br>Do not understand the reasons for such large staff reductions | Grasp how the company plans to return to a leadership position in the industry<br>Comprehend the decision rationale for staff reduction |
| **FEEL** | Worried about their own future and that of their families<br>Concerned for their friends who lost their jobs | Energized about their future with the company and the prospects for success<br>Reassured that the company has acted responsibly in separating employees |
| **DO** | Frozen and not engaging in work or the change effort | Recommitted to the company and to fully join in serving customers and helping the company regain its prominence |

For her presentation, the statement of her main idea is "We will regain market leadership through grit and creativity."

The questions surrounding this idea are largely "What?" and "How?" questions.

- What does grit mean?
- What do I need to do?
- How will we operationalize this?
- What do you mean by creativity?
- What is changing?
- Who will lead this effort?
- When will it happen?
- What is the impact on me?

She's selected the problem-solution pattern because, while her objective is to inspire, she doesn't want to sugar coat the reality of the situation. Based on her analysis of the audience, she believes they want to hear an honest assessment of the situation and what Cheryl plans to do to tackle the company's challenges. Cheryl also completed the journalist's grid for her presentation:

| WHAT IS CHANGING? | New formations and new messaging that is aligned to our customers' priorities. |
|---|---|
| WHAT DO YOU NEED TO DO? | Master our new messaging, because we must differentiate ourselves. |
| WHAT DOES GRIT MEAN? | Our ability to execute. A good plan without execution will fail. |

Your HINT-based storyboard is the foundation of your presentation. To be sure that you build the best possible base, I recommend adhering to the following psychological principles outlined in Stephen Kosslyn's book *Clear and to the Point: 8 Psychological Principles for Compelling PowerPoint Presentations*:

# Make Sure It's Relevant

Communication is most effective when neither too much nor too little information is presented. There are two main aspects of this principle:

- Each slide is a message package. They should always be built around the take-home message. Every piece of information should be relevant to the main idea.
- The audience should be told only what they need in order to understand the message.

*Ask Yourself:* Do the slide's headline and visual help convey the message? Do they contain the relevant information that the audience needs to understand the message? If the answer to either of these questions is no, you should rethink your slide.

# Don't Overload Your Audience

Presentations often require viewers to take in a large amount of material over multiple slides. The **principle of capacity limitations** states that people have a limited capacity to retain and to process information and so will not understand a message if too much information must be retained or processed. You should account for this in your slides by doing the following:

- Don't overload slides. This will overwhelm your audience's capacity to retain the information and distract from your presentation. One idea per slide.
- Keep visuals simple: Asking your audience to interpret a complex table or graph will overload them with information.

*Ask Yourself:* Will my slides make my audience do too much work, to the point where they won't have the capacity to both interpret the slide and listen to what I'm trying to say? If so, you should rethink the slide.

## Chapter 7 Key Takeaways

- Use the HINT method (headline, image, notes, transition) to create your storyboard.
- Index cards and a pencil help you think visually. Don't start in PowerPoint.
- Think about a concept that can communicate your idea visually.
- It may take more than one card to convey a concept or idea. The audience isn't going to be counting your slides. If your case is compelling, they won't even realize they're looking at slides.
- Get a hole punch and a rubber band, put a hole in the upper-left corner, and loop the rubber band through—now you can go through your cards and review the flow anytime and anywhere.
- Make sure everything on your slides is relevant to the audience.
- Don't overload your slides. Keep them simple.
- Don't neglect your transitions—they tie elements of a presentation together and give audiences direction.

# CHAPTER 8

# More on Opening and Concluding

Start strong, stay strong, finish strong by always
remembering why you're doing it in the first place.
—*Ralph Marston*

It would not be overexaggerating to say that the opening is the most critical part of the presentation—for several reasons. One of them is the **primacy effect**, a cognitive bias in which people tend to believe and remember what they hear first rather than what they hear later. There's a good reason for this: your audience's short-term memory is less "crowded" at the beginning of a presentation. As a result, it has more capacity for the mental functions like rehearsal, consolidation, and storage, which help transfer information to long-term memory. And as we've discussed, we want our audiences to remember our presentation messages for potential future action.

The opening is critical for another important reason. If the opening does not capture the audience's attention and answer some of the basic audience motivation questions we discussed earlier (such as "Will my time spent here be worth it to me?"), you run the risk of not fully engaging them with the rest of your presentation. You want the focus to be on you and your message, not their email, their upcoming meetings, or their dinner options.

# Elements of the Opening

Your opening should accomplish four goals. The first is capturing the audience's attention, and of the four, this one must come first. Then you must, in no particular order, orient the audience to the topic, establish credibility, and provide a road map for your presentation.

## CAPTURING THE AUDIENCE'S ATTENTION

Attention is a precious commodity. It is very difficult for a modern audience to focus for more than a brief amount of time. It's critical that you think carefully about how you can grab their attention and keep it. Let's look at this important goal from two perspectives— one is the content of your attention grabber, and the other is your approach to delivery. Your opening attention grabber should have good content—this could be a relevant anecdote, a memorable statistic, or a meaningful quote. You might begin with a striking visual or a thought-provoking rhetorical question. Any of these common methods of capturing attention can work, depending on your topic. A little research and due diligence will help you find the right attention-getting strategy.

The other perspective that you need to consider is the importance of first impressions on your audience. In a 1993 study, social psychologists Nalini Ambady and Robert Rosenthal videotaped thirteen graduate students teaching their individual classes.[1] Then they took three random ten-second clips and combined them into one thirty-

---

1    N. Ambady & R. Rosenthal, "Half a Minute: Predicting Teacher Evaluations from Thin Slices of Nonverbal Behavior and Physical Attractiveness," *Journal of Personality and Social Psychology* 64, no. 3 (1933): 431–441. https://doi.org/10.1037/0022-3514.64.3.431.

second clip that summed up the teaching of each student. Their peers then watched the clips and rated the graduate fellows on thirteen unique variables, such as "active," "competent," and "confident." Ambady and Rosenthal combined these individual scores into a single rating for each graduate instructor and correlated them with the teachers' student ratings from the end of the semester.

Before I give you the results, here's some context: In social psychology, any correlation over 0.6 in a study is considered very strong. Can you guess what correlation Ambady and Rosenthal found between the video and the end-of-semester rating? It was 0.76! It's stunning how accurate those predictions were. Ambady and Rosenthal concluded that humans tend to make judgments based on narrow "slices" of experience—anywhere from ten to thirty seconds. They named this phenomenon **thin-slicing**, and it's critical to understand it when you're opening your presentation. Combined with the primacy effect we discussed earlier, how you open your presentation will be one of the thin slices your audience remembers best, so it is crucial to make a strong first impression.

In a professional setting, there is nothing wrong with the standard introduction: "Hi, I'm Tommy Re with Vital Talent. Thank you for inviting me to talk with you today." But it's also boring and predictable. Why waste the brief few seconds of your opening with that? Remember, your opening is when the audience is making their very early assessments of you. It could be good to disrupt the tape that's likely playing in their head—the one that's going, "Okay, I'm going to be sitting through another ordinary presentation." So, what can you do in the opening that will help generate interest and help you advance your purpose?

> **It is crucial to make a strong first impression.**

You don't even need to say anything to generate interest. In fact, sometimes silence is more powerful than anything you can say. I tried this at the beginning of one of my presentations about how to effectively manage in a matrix-type organization. A matrixed management system has complex reporting structures. Managers have direct reports, but they also have management responsibility for people on projects they lead. This type of organizational structure can often lead to competing priorities. And it's often difficult for managers to be effective. My presentation was designed to introduce ways to successfully manage in that environment.

In drafting my opening, I thought about a Rubik's cube as an analogy. It has layers with a complex structure just like a matrixed organization. I thought, *If you have a method, you can solve it,* which was like the main message of my presentation: if you have a thought-out approach, you can manage in a matrix more easily. So, I brought a Rubik's cube into the conference room with me. As I waited for the room to fill up, I stood up front and just worked on the tough puzzle. I didn't say anything. I just immersed myself in solving the multi-colored contraption. Finally, with everyone present, I could tell that they were all curious about why I was doing a Rubik's cube. Putting down the toy, I looked at them and said, "Managing in a matrixed organization is like solving a Rubik's cube …" That simple gesture got their attention and set up the rest of the session for success.

Now, your opening doesn't need to be as dramatic as that one. (Although it couldn't hurt!) It can be simple or subtle, but above all else, it must be intentional. A good opening lays the foundation for an engaging presentation. Once you've done that, there are a few more things you need to do in the opening.

## ORIENTING THE AUDIENCE

People go in and out of meetings all day. Sometimes they only have a cursory understanding of why they are even there. If you don't believe me, just tune in to some of the premeeting chatter in your next few meetings. You may hear things like "What is this meeting about?" or "Who called this meeting?" All of which translate to "Why am I here?" If you're giving your presentation at a meeting, you need to include an orientation to set the context for your audience. Show them where you're going to take them in your presentation so they don't think this is just another meeting they can zone out in.

This is an opportunity to use the work you did in understanding the communication situation to benefit the audience. In your orientation, you must remind the audience of the problem that you are there to solve. The orientation portion of your opening should not take long. It's like an agenda review at the opening of a meeting or the learning objectives at the beginning of a training session. Make your orientation intriguing and compelling. This is a great opportunity to be creative and orient the audience with a thought-provoking but illustrative visual.

## ESTABLISHING CREDIBILITY

Your next goal is to establish credibility. This, as we discussed earlier, is what Aristotle referred to as ethos. Credibility relies on many factors, one of which is the speaker's subject matter expertise. In general, we tend to trust in experts. We listen to doctors for medical advice, interior designers for home decor. And you may attribute more credibility to Bobby Flay when he talks about food than if he were giving a presentation on physics. (Sorry, Bobby, if you know more about physics than I thought. Nevertheless, I'd listen to any talk you give on cooking!)

Another aspect of credibility comes from a speaker's character. Of course, some elements of character, like reputation, precede the speaker. If you have seen your parish priest serve the poor and needy in your community, you'll be more inclined to believe him when he takes the pulpit to give a homily on the Gospels. But other elements of credibility emerge from the presenter's in-the-moment behavior. This has to do with the speaker's style.

In one of my favorite books, *How to Talk So People Listen*, communication consultant Sonya Hamlin discusses how people react to different speaking styles. In her research, she found that people react positively to speakers who are friendly, warm, and interesting. This is a matter of how you "land" on people. You come across as friendly and warm when you smile, make eye contact, and have open body language.

The famous Nixon-Kennedy debates of 1960 illustrate just how intuitively we pick up on things like warmth. But more importantly, it demonstrates the outsized impact presence has on speaker credibility. From a purely argumentative standpoint, Nixon won the debate: his answers were detailed and specific, and he made several strong points in his exchanges with Kennedy. But according to a survey taken after the debate, those who watched the televised version believed Kennedy won. Audiences were drawn to the warmth in his speaking style. Even though his answers were vaguer than Nixon's, Kennedy carried himself with charisma and confidence. We'll cover much more about speaker style later in the book.

## PROVIDING A ROAD MAP

Your fourth and final goal for the opening is to provide a preview or road map for the audience. This is a little different from setting the context. You can think of setting the context as the Google satellite image of the presentation—very zoomed out. The road map, on the other hand, provides turn-by-turn directions on how to arrive at a destination. In the opening, you need to lay out the route that you'll take and then refer back to that route during the presentation.

Why? Well, while adults like autonomy and control, they give up those things when they give a speaker their attention. Our brain is a pattern seeker and a problem solver—it wants to know what's coming. Just think about the last time you were on a plane that wasn't moving on the tarmac, and no one was giving you a reason for the delay in getting you to your destination. If you're like me, your skin was probably crawling, even though you were sitting calmly in your seat. If you're a presenter, you don't want your audience to waste their precious mental energy wondering where they're going and how you're going to get them there. That's why we give them a preview—a road map. A visual aid works well here: not only does it simplify information, but it can also provide built-in signposts to show where you are in the journey and where you're headed next.

## Concluding

Just as it's important to get the opening right because of the primacy effect, it's also important to get the conclusion right because of the **recency bias**. This is our tendency to remember things that happen most recently compared to things that happen earlier. In essence, your opening and conclusion are prime opportunities for you to stick in your audience's memory. Let's examine the purpose of the conclusion and a few techniques for making your conclusion powerful and memorable.

### THE PURPOSE OF THE CONCLUSION

The three objectives of the conclusion are as follows:

- Provide logical and emotional closure for the audience

- Summarize your key points or takeaways
- Reiterate and reinforce your purpose

Closure and resolution are important concepts in reasoning and storytelling. From a logical perspective, you want to present or reiterate a conclusion to make sense of the premises that were described. Imagine a comedian sets up a great joke and then leaves the stage before the punch line. It's just not fair! We crave that closure. Worst of all, imagine how you would feel if you're watching a great play or movie and you never find out what happens to the heroine. We need to know what happened! Audiences seek closure and resolution, so don't leave yours without good ones.

Remember those key points or insights that you worked so hard on earlier in the development process? They are now going to be your summary points in the conclusion. You are going to repeat them now to solidify them in your audience's memory. Repetition of the key message is important because repetition activates memory. In an oral presentation, we want to activate a type of memory known as **gist memory**. Psychologists have discovered that people form two types of memories: verbatim and gist. Verbatim memories are the word-for-word copies of things you learned in the past. Your times tables are a good example of

> **Audiences seek closure and resolution, so don't leave yours without good ones.**

verbatim memories. Gist memories, while less accurate, capture the topic's general meaning or "essence," as we discussed earlier.

Here's what's interesting: gist memories tend to last longer than verbatim memories! In an oral presentation, you don't expect the audience to remember every detail—that's why you may have handouts. You want to use the power of the live presentation to work on seeding the essence of your message and the few very important things you want the audience to know, feel, or do. Throughout your presentation, you expose your audience to certain concepts, ideas, proofs, and arguments. In the conclusion, you're reinforcing those points and building a feeling of familiarity with them so the audience can process them in short-term memory and eventually convert them into long-term memory.

Finally, the conclusion is when you reiterate the ultimate purpose of your presentation. You can reestablish context and, in doing so, land a key piece of knowledge, appeal to a common emotion, or make a call to action. As you work out your conclusion, you need to come back to your overarching purpose. If you laid out a compelling reason for listening in your opening, you must return to that reason now, having proven its worth. Then you must set in your audience's mind the final, clear, and resonant sound of meaning.

## HOW TO CRAFT A CONCLUSION

Let's look at crafting your conclusion by returning to our three major presentation purposes: to inform, to persuade, or to inspire. If you are informing, like Chuck, you'll want to take a **descriptive** approach to your conclusion. Remember that an informative presentation seeks to increase the level of knowledge an audience has about a topic. During the presentation, you've established key points and takeaways with solid evidence and explanations. In the conclusion, you need to summarize the evidence and make those key points clear. Finally, you need to encourage the audience to internalize the new information you've provided.

If you are giving a persuasive presentation, you can use a **pre-scriptive** approach to the conclusion. Here you remind the audience of what you want them to do. Your key summary points may be designed around the reason to act and the way to take action. If you are asking the audience members to approve the budget for a new product, you'll focus on why the new product will help the company achieve its financial goals and how the funds will be used to get the product development completed. Then you will make your final appeal for action. It can be as simple as "I ask that you approve our request during the upcoming budget meeting." At this point, there is no mystery in what you want the audience to do. As intuitive as this may seem, you'd be surprised at how many persuasive presentations I see where there is no ask. Maybe some presenters think it's too simple to flat out ask, so they convolute their endings to make them sound more sophisticated. Don't do that. Be direct. Ask for action. You'll be delighted at the clarity of the response you will get. And even if you don't get the outcome you want, you'll know exactly where you stand. You can use the information in that rejection to revise your proposal.

When you are giving an inspirational presentation, you can use a **reflective** approach to the conclusion. A reflective approach asks the audience to think deeply about the topic. You can incorporate an emotional appeal to help this happen. If you end your presentation with a moving story that touches the audience's heart, they will likely reflect on that emotion or topic. Think about how often we do that. Watch interviews of athletes after winning a big championship: they are filled with emotion and reflect on the meaning of the event and the work it took to achieve the win. Remember when you received a less-than-expected grade on an exam? After the initial feeling of disappointment or anger, you likely reflected on that disappointment to see what went wrong and what you could do better next time. Reflection helps us make change, and the purpose of an inspirational presentation, as we discussed earlier, is to help with internal change and influence how someone feels about something.

A frequent piece of advice I give to presenters is to work out your conclusion in as much detail as possible and then commit it to memory. The reason is simple. It's the last thing your audience will hear, and it's likely the part of your presentation they'll remember most, along with the opening. The tools and resources available to you in putting together your conclusion are similar to those you used in your opening. You can use an anecdote, statistics, rhetorical question, quote, or challenge. The key is to find the approach that fits your presentation type and purpose. Make it meaningful, and make it memorable.

## Chapter 8 Key Takeaways

- The opening and closing are the most critical parts of your presentation.
- In the opening, you capture attention, orient the audience, establish credibility, and provide a road map for your audience.
- Conclusions have three objectives: provide logical and emotional closure, summarize your key takeaways, and reinforce or restate your purpose.
- Use one of three approaches to the conclusion—descriptive, prescriptive, or reflective.
- Work out your opening and conclusion in as much detail as possible, and commit it to memory.

CHAPTER 9

# What You'll Say—the Language of Your Presentation

Words are sacred. If you get the right ones in the
right order, you can nudge the world a little.

—*Tom Stoppard*

A presentation is not a speech, but what you say is just as important. There are many ways to prepare what you're going to say when presenting. There is no right way. There is only one imperative. The audience must be able to follow and understand you. This seems straightforward, but I've seen many presenters stumble at this point in their presentation development, and it shows up in their delivery. It's because they take one of two extreme approaches. First, some don't prepare any words at all, and they wing it. They rely on the slides and just ad lib. What results is usually too many words, disjointed logic, and far too many *ums*, *ahs*, and every other verbal filler in the book.

The other approach is that they prepare and memorize a script. At first glance, this seems like a good strategy, and it can be a very helpful way of getting at the precise language you want to use. The challenge, of course, is internalizing the script or delivering it as if you are speaking spontaneously. While this approach might yield a more coherent verbal presentation, the speaker needs great performance skills to pull it off. The most boring approach (and the deadliest) is what I see most often. It's when a presenter reads the text from their slides, word for word. And if they've designed poor slides, there are probably too many words on the screen. I don't recommend this approach, as it completely negates the power that comes with a dual-channel presentation. It's a one-way ticket to boring your audience.

A better approach is somewhere in between the extremes of true improvisation and rote memorization. It's when a presenter has carefully thought through language choices but with enough breathing room to sound spontaneous. Writing a word-for-word script isn't necessary for informal presentations. In fact, the ability to be flexible and address questions during your presentation and effortlessly jump back into your organized flow is a valuable skill. For more formal presentations, like TED Talks, earnings calls, legal proceedings, or other communication situations where exactness is required, scripting could be useful, but the presenter must make sure it doesn't sound like a rote memorization.

## How to Work with Words and Slides

You'll want to create talking points for each slide. This is where the notes in the HINT model are important. Remember, if you've designed your slides well, there won't be too much text on the slide for the audience to read. They're seeing the visually stimulating billboard for your slide's message. It's your job as the presenter to add to what they're seeing by explaining, describing, interpreting, reinforcing, or synthesizing.

A great technique to keep your script and slides in sync is to go back to the cards you created for your HINT storyboard. The back of the card where you made your initial notes is the perfect place to add your key talking points. An additional benefit of using the cards is that they give you a guide for balancing the verbal and visual content for each slide. If you have two pages of script for one slide, you're not going to keep the audience's visual attention. You must keep the level of visual interest up by creating a dynamic presentation that grabs your audience's eyes and ears.

Here's what I mean: Let's say you have four minutes of commentary and two slides. That's two minutes of talking per slide. Presenting for two minutes with nothing happening on screen is a long time! Modern audiences are in the habit of seeing more interesting and dynamic visuals. Turn on your favorite TV show or movie, watch for four minutes, and count the number of cuts you see. (A cut is just a change of camera angle or the camera's point of view.) In every cut, the audience sees something slightly different. Each TV show will vary, but my guess is there will be close to one hundred cuts. Now, I'm not suggesting that you have one hundred slides for a four-minute presentation, but you do want to have your slides match your verbal talking points. Again, this is a presentation, not a speech.

A great way to practice this balance of commentary and slides is to try the PechaKucha style of presenting. PechaKucha is a storytelling format where a presenter shows twenty slides for twenty seconds of commentary each. It was inspired by Astrid Klein and Mark Dytham of Tokyo's Klein-Dytham Architecture. In the culture of their firm, they had a desire to "talk less, show more" in their presentations. This drove them to create the PechaKucha format in February 2003, where presenters were restricted to presenting twenty seconds for each of their twenty slides. While I don't think all business presentations can be six minutes and forty seconds long (although I'm sure many audiences would like it), the idea of rapidly changing visuals corresponding to key points and ideas is compelling. I think it captures the sentiment of Nancy Duarte, designer and author of *Slide:ology*, who likes to say, "Slides are free!" I love it and enthusiastically recommend her work to you!

As you're developing your talking points, you can determine where you want to use precise language and incorporate a particular word or phrase. Or you can give yourself more latitude in the words you choose in the moment and just note the key takeaways you want the audience to remember. Keep in mind that, unlike a speech where everything relies on the spoken word, a presentation is a combination of visual and verbal communication, so you don't need to rely solely on the spoken word for memorability.

As you are developing your specific language choices, incorporate micro scripts—short phrases that capture the essence of something in a memorable way. These beats of action were first described in Bill Schley's book *The Micro-Script Rules*, and it's a powerful way to impart key information to your audience. Micro scripts are often used in advertising. Think of "melts in your mouth, not in your hand" or "the quicker picker upper." There's a good chance you remember the brands associated with those micro scripts as well—M&Ms and Bounty paper towels. Jingles are also a form of micro script: you probably can hum the tones for "like a good neighbor, State Farm is there." But micro scripts can be used for more than just commercials. One of the most memorable high-stakes micro scripts was used by the defense attorney Johnnie Cochran in the trial of O. J. Simpson: "If the glove doesn't fit, you must acquit."

Micro scripts aren't new. They're merely a modern name for a rhetorical device. There are many rhetorical devices—far too many to review in this book. If you'd like to learn more about them, read *Writing with Clarity and Style: A Guide to Rhetorical Devices for Con-*

*temporary Writers*, by Robert A. Harris. They are an element of language style. Language style is the way you arrange the words you say. It's what transforms the information and data of your idea into *your* **compelling** messages that the audience wants to listen to.

Style and rhetorical devices are more than ornamentation. They are a means of helping your audience understand and remember your message. And I believe they separate the average presenter from the truly

> **They are a means of helping your audience understand and remember your message.**

exceptional. Think back to some of the best presentations you've attended. My guess is the presenter used these powerful devices to capture your attention. For our purposes, let's focus on five of the most useful rhetorical devices for business presentations: analogy, examples, metaphor, parallelism, and rhetorical questions. It's a good idea to include several in your presentation.

# Rhetorical Devices

## ANALOGY

An analogy makes use of something already well known to explain something that is less well known. Analogies are useful in informative and persuasive presentations because they help your audience quickly understand exactly what you mean. For example, when Chuck is discussing the new drug's mechanism of action, he might say, "Think of it like the filter you would find in a water purification system" to describe its function to those in his audience who aren't aware of the complex scientific terms that make the drug work.

## EXAMPLES

Examples help illustrate your point. They're so important and familiar that you may not have realized that they're considered a rhetorical device. Examples should be relevant to your topic and drawn from the real world. Always make sure your examples are plausible. You don't want your audience debating their plausibility in their minds. Good examples help build strong arguments. In persuading her audience to do business with her, Amanda might use examples of how Activate's solution has helped other well-known companies.

## METAPHORS

A metaphor speaks to one thing as if it were another. Metaphors help listeners understand complex or abstract ideas by using more familiar terms. They can also help to drive past the literal truth and hit on the emotional and psychological truth. Here's how Cheryl might use a metaphor in describing how it feels to struggle to achieve a sales goal: "I know it feels like we're at the bottom of Everest right now and there's a hard and grueling journey ahead of us."

## PARALLEL CONSTRUCTION

Parallelism is particularly important for oral presentations. It refers to using the same general structure for multiple parts of a sentence (or for multiple sentences) to link them together. Parallelism provides a sense of overall cohesion. We often see this device used in formal speeches. Most Americans treasure the parallel expression in Abraham Lincoln's Gettysburg Address when he says, "that government, of the people, by the people, and for the people, shall not perish from the earth." It's poetic and easy to listen to, but more importantly, it is *memorable*. Rhythm and rhyme are incredibly important for the spoken word. Just because you're giving a business presentation and not a commemorative address, it doesn't mean you can't use them. Here's an example of a parallel construction that Amanda could use in her pitch: "We build our programs with research and data, we build our programs with rock-solid technology, and we build our programs with the most talented people in the industry."

## RHETORICAL QUESTION

A rhetorical question is one in which the answer is implied. Rhetorical questions give the presenter the opportunity to highlight something already known. Rhetorical questions are usually phrased in a way that requires a yes or no answer. Of course, you always want to be sure the audience will answer the way you like. And don't overuse rhetorical questions. After all, they can become tedious, can't they?

# Some Language Considerations to Avoid

As we've discussed, many of your language choices will be driven by the audience and what they know and understand. Now, let's look at some choices you should avoid because they can confuse or overwhelm your audience. They can conveniently be condensed into the simple ABCs: acronyms, buzzwords, and complex language.

## ACRONYMS

A.k.a. CIA. LBJ. JFK. While you might think you know what these acronyms stand for, have I made it explicitly clear? Avoid undefined acronyms, because they sow confusion and create chaos. They can alienate your audience and make your message difficult to understand. If there are acronyms in your presentation, define them first so your audience understands them. Earlier we discussed the concept of speaker credibility, and to some extent, knowing the language shortcuts the audience members use can be a sign that you know your audience. That's only true, however, with a homogeneous audience. If your audience members come from various industries or departments, it is unlikely that they know each other's acronyms. In addition to making your message more obscure, using acronyms that are unfamiliar to some members of the group sets up an unnecessary "in-group" dynamic that can impact decision-making behavior.

## BUZZWORDS

In our workshops, we have fun with buzzwords, jargon, and clichés. One activity is to list the terms and phrases that could be considered "corporate speak," and let me tell you, these lists are long! We all laugh when we hear "moving the needle," "raising the bar," "thinking outside the box" and "let me socialize that" listed out. But we all are guilty of using them! I know I am. These overused phrases have lost their impact, and they often obscure rather than clarify meaning. When you're working on your notes, be mindful of the words you choose. Look for ways to articulate the concept without leaning on clichés.

## COMPLEX LANGUAGE

If you're reading this book, I'm guessing there's a part of you that loves language or at least appreciates the power of language. Effective use of language can give your presentation power and memorability. But if you use language to try to impress your audience or make yourself sound intelligent, you run the risk of alienating them. People don't like to feel spoken down to, so don't complicate your message with unnecessary language.

> **A leader's job is to make the vague clear, the complex simple, and the abstract concrete.**

When I work with leaders, we discuss the power of language, and I remind them that a leader's job is to make the vague clear, the complex simple, and the abstract concrete. And that takes work. You need to think hard about word choice and avoid complex language. Remember, your goal is to help your audience understand you, not marvel at your vocabulary. Choose simpler words when speaking. Don't say *expeditious* when you can say *fast* or *parameters* when you mean *limits*. Simpler and shorter words just lighten the cognitive load. For more ideas on how to make your writing more effective, see our *Plain and Simple Business Writing* ebook.

## Message Spices

In addition to the rhetorical devices we just discussed, there are other "message spices" that you should consider when drafting your presentation. **Message spices** are ways to make your presentation more engaging and interactive—and the best presenters know how and when to employ them.

### HUMOR

Humor is a powerful way to engage your audience. It lightens the mood and communicates a sense of familiarity that can help build rapport. You should, however, be careful how and why you employ humor. For example, you wouldn't want to open a serious meeting about underperformance or job cuts with jokes about firing people. I'd recommend thinking about humor as a means of connecting with the audience on a more personal and human level rather than just trying to be funny. That doesn't mean you can't be funny. Anecdotes, self-effacing humor, and wittiness can be a fun and inviting way to engage the audience.

Even if you're not telling jokes, it's important to carefully consider the humorous stories you plan to include and how they connect you to your audience. You never want to risk alienating your audience. If you feel your anecdotes have even a slight chance of doing that, just leave them out. Also, consider your communication situation!

You have more latitude with humor, for example, in an after-dinner address or on a celebratory occasion, such as when a colleague retires or achieves a milestone. But for most business presentations, good humor is more about connection than laughter.

## AUDIENCE INVOLVEMENT

Business presentations, more than any other type of public speaking, are suited for audience involvement. You can invite your audience into the conversation rhetorically, as we discussed earlier, or directly. Rhetorical questions and reflective questions engage the audience's brains—they make them think, ponder, and question. Let's say you're an HR director and you're presenting to the senior leadership team on the need for a new coaching program for your organization. Asking "How have you benefited from coaching during your career?" is an open-ended question that will get your audience psychologically engaged even if they don't verbalize an answer. That question has the added value of introducing a personal and emotional dimension that will be sure to get their attention.

# Chapter 9 Key Takeaways

- Preparing what you'll say is critical for crisp and clear delivery. You don't need a word-for-word script, but you do need a good set of talking points in your HINT notes.
- Match the amount of talk time with your visuals, and keep them in sync.
- Incorporate rhetorical devices to capture the ear of your audience and to help illustrate your key points.
- Avoid corporate speak. Use clear and simple language.

# CHAPTER 10

# Making It Look Good

Slides are free.

—*Nancy Duarte*

We live in a visual world. Television, film, Pinterest, Facebook, and Instagram are now commonplace. We look at visuals on our screens all day. In fact, according to global tech care company Asurion, Americans look at their phones ninety-six times a day.[2] That's once every ten minutes. Almost five billion videos are watched on YouTube every single day.[3] Traditional newspapers and books filled with text are now just one of many ways to consume information and learn. And it's no surprise given that humans learn better from images than from text alone. This is due to a phenomenon known as the **picture-superiority effect**. When combined with text, pictures stimulate our brains twice: as verbal code and as image code. This code travels down

---

2    Asurion, "Americans Check Their Phones 96 Times a Day," Cision PR Newswire, November 21, 2019, https://www.prnewswire.com/news-releases/americans-check-their-phones-96-times-a-day-300962643.html.

3    Danny Donchev, "40 Mind Blowing YouTube Facts, Figures and Statistics—2022," FortuneLords, June 12, 2022, https://fortunelords.com/youtube-statistics/.

two different types of neural pathways[4] instead of just one, which means we are more likely to internalize both what the pictures look like and what they symbolize. For this reason, visuals are essential to communicating important concepts in presentations.

Think about presentations you've seen with nothing but walls of text. How much of those presentations do you remember? On the other hand, if you see a presentation with eye-catching visuals, your brain will have something to latch on to when you recall the presentation later—a bar graph with a simple caption and color scheme, or a photo used to demonstrate a humorous analogy. Text spells out your ideas, but visuals make those ideas look interesting. Your slides are maps for your audience. They use words and pictures to help get them somewhere. That somewhere is *insight* and *learning*.

Once you've crafted the verbal language of your presentation, you'll want to start working on the visual language of your presentation. Robert E. Horn, communication scholar and author of *Visual Language: Global Communication for the 21st Century*, defines visual language as

> **What people see is as important as what they hear.**

"the integration of words, images, and shapes into a single communication unit." Earlier, when you used the HINT model to create your storyboard, you worked hard to sketch out a visual that will help the audience understand your message. It's time now to design your visuals so they have the maximum impact.

Throughout this book, we've explained how presentations are a multi-channel learning experience. What people see is as important as what they hear. With the audience looking at you and your slides for the

---

4    A. J. O. Whitehouse, M. T. Maybery, and K. Durkin, "The Development of the Picture-Superiority Effect," *British Journal of Developmental Psychology* 24 (2006): 767–773. https://doi-org.prox.lib.ncsu.edu/10.1348/026151005X74153.

duration of the presentation, it'll be useful for you to know how to enhance your presentation power with visuals.

## Types of Visuals

Visuals help make the abstract more concrete. They transcend language and fluency barriers and make it easier to connect with diverse audiences. When used well, visuals help reduce complexity, which is why they are important for explaining subject matter that's unfamiliar. Using visuals to explain a process or concept is much easier than using words alone. Look at the table below. The words on the left describe the same thing as the image on the right. Which is quicker and easier to comprehend?

| A woody perennial plant having a single usually elongate main stem generally with few or no branches on its lower part |  |
| --- | --- |

But images alone aren't enough. Sometimes we need text and images together for a complete message. Here's what I mean. This familiar image without text just points one direction.

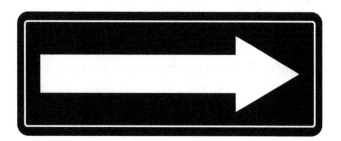

The words *ONE WAY* alone tell us only that there is one way to go, but not which way.

It isn't until they are combined that they form a complete visual message with all the important information we need to avoid getting hit by an oncoming truck!

## TYPES OF SLIDE VISUALS

The visuals we use in slide development come in four categories: images, charts and graphs, text, and symbols.

### *Images*

Pictures and illustrations are powerful. Pictures convey emotion, and illustrations help reduce complexity. The key to using pictures and illustrations well is to select the right one for the message you are trying to communicate or the point you want to support. For example, you may be recommending a policy where managers spend more one-on-one time with employees, providing coaching and feedback. You argue that when managers spend more intentional and meaningful time with employees, they create a shared sense of trust and employees feel more engaged and connected to the organization. An image of two people interacting in conversation or looking at a document together supports the underlying message in your presentation about the importance of the human connection.

There are countless ways to obtain quality images for your presentations. One method is using photos that you or someone in your company takes. Many companies have a library of marketing photos that might be useful on your slides. You can also purchase images from sites like Getty Images, 123RF, or iStock Photo. There are also several sites that offer free images, like Pexels and Unsplash. Even Microsoft PowerPoint now includes access to hundreds of images and icons for free. There's no excuse for you to have a blank slide!

On our website, www.talentisvital.com, we've provided a list of the many sites that have photographs and illustrations, both free and for purchase. As a note, remember that the photographs and images may have copyright and licensing terms that you must adhere to.

## CHARTS AND GRAPHS

For many of you, charts and graphs will be the mainstay of your visual presentations because they are the primary vehicle for presenting data. You may be sharing data about the results of an experiment, depicting the growing budget deficit, or showing the findings of a customer satisfaction survey. The primary reason to use any chart is to show relationships more quickly and clearly than you can any other way. Charts and graphs show relationships, changes over time, or the makeup of something. They can also tell a story. In her magnificent book *Storytelling with Data*, Cole Nussbaumer Knaffic describes how presenters can shape their data into compelling stories to achieve their communication goals. We won't be going into the level of depth that Cole does in her books, but we will look at a few principles and ideas that can guide you in adding this important type of visual into your presentation when you need to make a point with data. Here are a few practical guidelines for incorporating charts and graphs in your presentation:

### *Match the Occasion*

Selecting the correct format to display your data is probably the most important decision you can make about your chart or graph. You want to choose a chart or graph type that will quickly show the key point and the relationship in the data that you want the audience to understand. Let's say Chuck has data about when subjects started in the trial. A frequency distribution using a column chart would be a much better choice than a pie chart. To make this simpler, I've listed five common relationship types and an example of the types of charts or graphs that would help convey the message. The following table will help you select the right chart for the comparison you're trying to make:

| | COMPONENT COMPARISON (SHOWS THE SIZE OF EACH PART AS A PERCENTAGE OF THE TOTAL) | ITEM COMPARISON (SHOWS HOW THINGS RANK) | TIME-SERIES COMPARISON (SHOWS HOW THINGS CHANGE OVER TIME) | FREQUENCY COMPARISON (SHOWS HOW THINGS FALL INTO A SERIES OF PROGRESSIVE NUMERICAL RANGES) | CORRELATION COMPARISON (SHOWS WHETHER THE RELATIONSHIP BETWEEN TWO VARIABLES FOLLOWS OR DOES NOT FOLLOW THE PATTERN YOU WOULD NORMALLY EXPECT) |
|---|---|---|---|---|---|
| PIE | X | | | | |
| BAR | | X | | | X |
| COLUMN | | | X | X | |
| LINE | | | X | X | |
| DOT | | | | | X |

### *Determine What's Most Important, and Emphasize It*

Your job as a presenter is to help your audience "get it." When we present data in charts and graphs, we need to make clear where we want them to focus by using preattentive attributes, design elements that help the audience make sense of your graph. Some examples of these are color, size, orientation, shape, line width, marks, and spatial position. Let's say you have four major customer segments, and you want to make a point about one of them—the pharmaceutical industry segment. You create a pie chart showing your customer segments,

> **Your job as a presenter is to help your audience "get it."**

but instead of using four colors to represent the major customer segments, you can use a shade of gray for the three segments you aren't focusing on and a brighter color for the pharmaceutical segment, the area you want to discuss. The audience's eyes will be immediately drawn there, and you'll lighten the cognitive load for them.

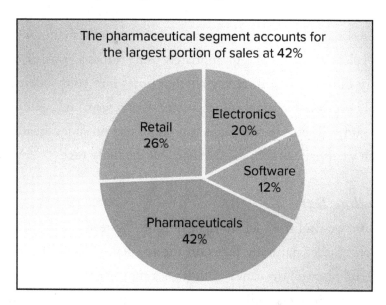

The pharmaceutical segment accounts for the largest portion of sales at 42%

### *Keep Your Charts Clear and Simple*

It's easy to put too much information in a chart. When you're giving a presentation and showing slides on a screen, you want to keep your charts simple and clean so that your audience can synthesize the data quickly. This means you need to identify the single most important message you want to communicate and design the chart to convey that information. Unlike in a written document, your audience won't have that much time to delve into complex data while you're presenting. Depending on the venue, they may not even be able to see smaller details. Leave those specific graphs for a leave-behind document such as a white paper or a Slidedoc, where your audience can really delve into the data. In the presentation, however, you want to be intentional about what you're showing them.

### *Text*

Text is a form of visual communication. It's something we look at onscreen and, as we saw in the example of the one-way sign, it's an important component in conveying your message. Sadly, the path of least resistance for many presenters is to use text as the main (or only) visual element on a slide. Appropriately using text as a visual element is very different than dumping all your notes into your slides. Text should provide important information *and* add visual stimulation to your slides. There are two primary types of text on slides: **headline**, which we usually find in the title bar, and the **body text**.

### *Headline Text*

Because we read from left to right in most Western countries, your audience's eyes naturally focus on the top left of the slide. It is a powerful place on the canvas. But it's not the only place you can put a headline. Business audiences that see the same slide structure over and over can become lulled into a sense of complacency and boredom. So, to shake it up and grab their attention, do something very simple: just move the headline.

As you build your presentation, experiment with putting your headline in different places on your slide. You can put it at the center left of the slide with an image on the right side. Or you can use an image that occupies the entire slide with the headline at the bottom. Take risks! Be creative! By varying your slide layout, you keep your audience stimulated. The key is to make the headline stand out. You can do this by using a larger font size or even a different color. Regardless of your approach, your headline text needs to pack a punch.

### Body Text

You should be just as intentional with your body text. Body text should never overcrowd your slide or convey the entirety of what you're going to say in your presentation. Try to avoid using bulleted lists if possible. They are a trap that can put your audience to sleep. Here are a few thoughts on using body text on your slides.

### Limit It

I've mentioned this several times in this book, but it bears repeating—presenters should not read the body text word for word on their slides. We've all seen it, and usually the slide they are reading from is totally overcrowded with full sentences. Your audience can read. This is a design issue. The best way to think about body text is to limit it. Keep slide text to a short phrase, or even a single word, that you will expand upon in your oral presentation. Remember, your slides are a visual aid to your presentation; they are not a document designed to be read independently.

## *Use Legible Font*

As fun as cool fonts can be, I recommend sticking to classic sans serif fonts. Sans serif fonts don't have the little "feet" or serifs you see in type fonts used in written text like newspapers. Times New Roman, for example, is a serif font. Fonts like Arial, Verdana, Franklin Gothic, and Twentieth Century are bolder and easier to read on a screen at a moment's glance. Also, make sure your font size is large enough for the entire audience to clearly read. Nothing is more annoying to an audience than not being able to read something on a slide. Test out your font sizes with your screen and room size. If you're presenting virtually, you have more flexibility with font size, as the screen will be closer to your audience. And you shouldn't use more than three fonts per presentation. One for headlines, one for body text, and one that can be used sparingly for special impact.

## *Concepts, Metaphors, and Diagrams*

A **diagram** is a collection of shapes and symbols that illustrate the interactions between the parts of a whole. It communicates abstract concepts that help your listeners understand something dynamic. Diagrams show movement—be it the operation of a supply chain or the structure of an org chart. They are a powerful way to explain a complicated real-world system in a short amount of time. They can even be a map. Here are some of the concepts that we often need to communicate through diagrams, as they are outlined in Nancy Duarte's excellent book *Slide:ology: The Art and Science of Creating Great Presentations*:

- **How Things Flow**: For example, do they flow in a circular fashion or a linear fashion? Do they diverge or converge? Are they multidirectional?

- **How Things Are Structured**: This includes matrices and layered or treelike structures. A common example is the organizational chart, with layers and branches that depict the hierarchy within a company.
- **How Things Are Clustered**: If certain things are interrelated, do they overlap? Or are they enclosed within something else? Are they linked together? Venn diagrams are a good example of this.
- **How Things Radiate**: Do they have channels that spread out from a certain point? Do they have a core? If I were explaining, for example, that completing a survey notifies several departments of my company, my diagram would include a "Survey" circle with arrows pointing toward the surrounding departments' names.
- **Pictorial Processes**: This is a broad category of diagrams that illustrate realistic (as opposed to abstract) processes, reveals, directions, locations, or influences. This includes everything from schematics to maps to cross-section diagrams.

## Principles of Effective Visual Communication on Slides

Okay, add images and text. Put a chart here and there. Throw in a good concept diagram, and you're all set. Simple, right? Not exactly. The visual aspect of communication is easy to get wrong. Poorly conceived visuals can detract from the core message and can even be misleading. To make sure your visuals don't stand in the way of you achieving your presentation's objective, I recommend adhering to the following psychological principles:

## RELEVANCE

Communication is most effective when just the right amount of information is presented—not too little and not too much. There are two main aspects of this principle when it comes to your slides:

- Slides should always be built around the take-home message. This means every piece of information is relevant to the main idea.
- The audience should only see what they need to see to understand the message.

*Ask Yourself:* Is the slide or visual relevant to my take-home message? Does my slide or visual contain information that the audience needs to have so that they can understand my message? If the answer is no to either of these questions, rethink your visual.

## APPROPRIATE KNOWLEDGE

Communication requires prior knowledge about pertinent concepts, jargon, and symbols. To reach an audience, you need to make your pitch at a level they will understand. Think about three factors as you draft your slide visuals:

- **Visual Language**: Think about your visual vocabulary as well as the complexity and structure of your presentation. Will your audience be familiar with the symbols and signs you use? This is particularly important in presentations given by technical professionals to nontechnical audiences.
- **Displays**: Consider what is universally understood. For example, a standard bar graph will likely be more easily understood by a wider audience than a box-and-whisker chart.
- **Concepts and Information**: Use the insights from your audience analysis to determine if they have prior knowledge

of your concepts. If not, include a slide explicitly explaining and introducing them. This principle requires you to strike a balance between assuming your audience knows too little and assuming your audience knows too much. If you assume they know too little, you may come across as boring and patronizing. Assume they know too much, and the information may go over their heads.

*Ask Yourself:* Will my audience understand the language, displays, and concepts I use on my slides? If not, include a slide explaining this information, or change it to something more digestible.

## SALIENCE

According to the ***principle of salience***, we automatically give our attention to the thing that sticks out or is different. Large perceptible differences on a slide are the most salient. Salience takes many forms. Animation and movement capture attention and direct the viewer. Attention can also be drawn to text by using different typefaces, colors, and sizes. Making the most important parts of a slide the most salient not only draws audience attention in the moment but also increases memory down the line.

Salience shouldn't be given to things that are irrelevant or unimportant. While it may be tempting to choose a brightly colored, object-filled slide background to add some eye candy to a presentation, conspicuous backgrounds and multicolored objects that capture the attention of viewers detract from the core message. Instead, guide the audience's attention by making the most important information on the slide the most salient.

With PowerPoint, you can call attention to text or pictures by sending them in from the side with animation or by making them brighter, larger, or louder. Conversely, you can make objects less salient and remove them from viewers' attention by making them only a shade or two different from the background color. This is called "graying out." We used this technique earlier when we grayed out portions of a pie chart to focus on the salient industry sector. These methods can be particularly helpful when highlighting a specific part of an outline or when building up a slide one part at a time.

*Ask Yourself*: What is visually emphasized in this slide? Is it the most important component? If not, you need to rethink your design.

## DISCRIMINABILITY

The **principle of discriminability** states that two things must differ by a large enough proportion, or they will not be distinguished. While salience can direct and hold attention, discriminability is crucial if you want audiences to recognize the change in the first place. In your slide deck, this means making sure the elements of your slides are easily distinguished from one another. Here are some examples:

- **Distinguish Titles, Body Text, and Captions**: Bolding your titles is one way of making sure your audience can distinguish a headline from the body text, which allows for easier interpretation of the slide.
- **Use Colors to Contrast**: Pick colors for text, background, and elements that adequately contrast each other so that the text is easily readable.
- **Use Large Enough Text**: Small text on a slide makes the letters difficult to distinguish from one another.

*Ask Yourself*: Can I visually distinguish all the important parts of my slide?

## COMPATIBILITY

A message is easiest to understand if its form is compatible with its meaning. This principle is best illustrated by what is known as the *Stroop effect*. John Ridley Stroop showed individuals the names of colors written in various colors. The word *red* was written in either red, blue, or green ink, and the same was done for the words *blue* and *green*. The participants were then asked to report the color of the ink, *not* the word they were reading. When there was a mismatch between the word and the color (e.g., the word *red* appeared in blue ink), people had more difficulty identifying the color and made more errors. This is because the text violated the *principle of compatibility*. The form and meaning weren't compatible, and this confused the audience and forced them to take longer to identify the necessary information.

In your slides, this means thinking critically about how you want elements of your slides to function and ensuring their form matches that function. Here are a couple of tips:

- Slide design should correspond to the content of your presentation. Slides with a floral background, for example, would not be appropriate for a defense contracting meeting.
- Symbols or icons should accurately represent what they're meant to represent.
- Typeface should match the content of your presentation. While we encourage all presenters to use a standard typeface, if you do use a more nontraditional typeface, ensure it matches the content of your presentation. For example, you wouldn't use a digital typeface (like the font on a stopwatch or dishwasher) in a presentation about ancient Greece.

- Graphs and charts should be chosen based on the type of data being displayed and the desired outcome. Refer to the "Charts and Graphs" section to choose the best graph/chart for your needs.

*Ask Yourself:* Do all elements of my slide correspond to the content of my presentation?

## INFORMATIVE CHANGE

This principle states that people expect changes in properties to carry information. There are two parts to the *principle of informative change*. The first is that we expect every auditory or visual change to mean something. For your slides, this means that a sudden change in color, background, or terminology will lead your audience naturally to assume that new information is being conveyed. If the changes are purely arbitrary, they will be led astray.

Secondly, every change in meaning should be conveyed by a perceptible change in appearance or sound. What audiences see and hear is ultimately what they will take away, and changes in what you say or show should signal them toward necessary information. For example, if part of a graph is a projection to the future, it should look different in some way from the part that summarizes actual historical data.

*Ask Yourself:* Do all stylistic changes in my slides correspond to changes in the type of information I want to underline?

## CAPACITY LIMITATION

Presentations often require viewers to take in a large amount of material over multiple slides. The *principle of capacity limitations* states that people have a limited capacity to retain and to process information. They will not understand a message if too much information must be retained or processed. You should account for this in your slides by doing the following:

- **Don't Overload Slides**: I said it once, and I'll say it again—do not overload your slides with paragraphs of text. This will overwhelm your audience's capacity to retain the information and distract from your presentation.
- **Keep Visuals Simple**: Asking your audience to interpret a complex table or graph will overload them with information.
- **Organize Hierarchically**: Hierarchical organization is easier for people to conceptualize (and therefore remember).
- **Use Clear Labels**: Choose labels instead of keys on graphs and charts—searching for keys distracts the audience from the main idea of the visual, and it keeps them from focusing on what you're saying.

*Ask Yourself*: Do any of my slides make my audience do too much work, to the point that they will not have the capacity to both interpret the slide and listen to what I'm trying to say?

## Adding Motion and Animation: Is It Worth the Effort?

Just as visuals can add new layers of meaning to text, motion brings new depth to visuals. How things move can aid the comprehension of and engagement with visual content. Motion tends to heighten our emotional responses to images. In a study comparing the responses of participants to moving and still versions of twenty-seven different images, researchers found that picture motion significantly increased stimulation. Picture motion also tended to prompt more heart rate deceleration, most likely reflecting a greater allocation of attention to the more arousing images. Additionally, positive images were experienced as more positive, and negative images as more negative, when the image contained motion. Visual formats have been shown to improve comprehension of detailed information, especially in financial decision-making.

So, use motion and animation, but use it while adhering to the other psychological principles we've discussed. PowerPoint and Keynote and Canva have powerful animation capabilities that allow nondesigners to add interest and visual stimulation to your presentations. Those same features used irresponsibly, however, will distract your audience and detract from your credibility.

## Picking Your Tools

When it's time to move your presentation from your index cards to a digital format, the options are getting better and better. I rely on PowerPoint or Keynote. More recently we have been using Canva, a cloud-based design tool that offers a wide variety of templates to make the design process easier. Whichever tool you prefer to use, make sure you take advantage of the most important features. The slide-sorter view is an example of this. It acts as your digital storyboard and helps you see the flow of your presentation quickly. Additionally, the notes view is where you can transfer the notes you created on your cards.

# Mini Scenarios

## CHUCK: SAMPLE SLIDES

---

**Study Recruitment**                    🔬 **Excel**

- Our recruitment rate increased in 5 out 6 months in the last half of last year
- We recruited 15 subjects in July by December we recruited 31
- The only month with a decrease from the previous month was August
- The increase in enrollment from July to December was over 100%

---

Why this slide doesn't work: The headline doesn't tell the audience much other than the topic. There is too much text on the slide. If Chuck reads the slide, the audience's attention will be fragmented–should they listen or try to follow the words on screen? The icon Chuck uses is clean and it does indicate an increase of something, but it doesn't provide any valuable information. Chuck should use a chart with the actual data.

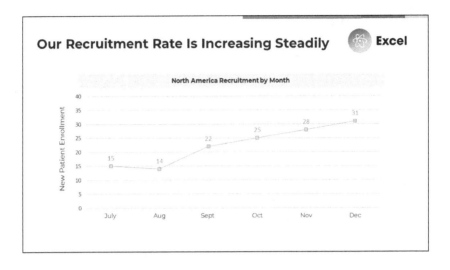

Why this slide works:

- Chuck uses a clean line chart that provides a variety of useful data in one visual.
- He is free to make several key points based on the audience's needs and interest.
- His headline is descriptive and gives the "so what" of the slide.

## AMANDA: SAMPLE SLIDES

**Our Process**

- Discovery
  - Interviews
  - Report
- Solution Development
  - Draft Core Messages
  - Design campaigns
  - Develop collateral
- Implementation
  - Build execution plan
  - Train marketing team

PROCESS
☑ STEP 1
☑ STEP 2
☑ STEP 3

◀ Activate

What doesn't work with this slide:

- The image on this slide is generic and doesn't provide any valuable information. It also takes up two-thirds of the slide real estate.
- The headline is topic based and non-descript. It doesn't give the audience any insight about the process.
- Amanda has kept the bullet points short, but they add no visual interest. They look like an outline and should be in her slide notes as talking points, not on the slide.

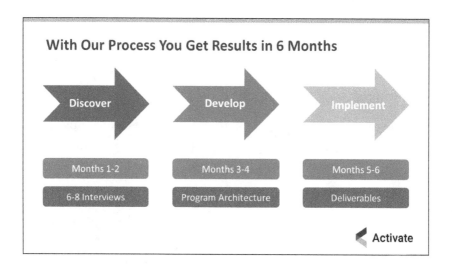

Why this slide works:

- The simple arrows show the three-step process and indicate a timeline.
- The shapes below the arrows provide additional detail about the duration of each phase.
- Amanda uses the pre-attentive attribute of color to provide the focus of each phase.
- Her headline summarizes the important elements of her message.

## CHERYL: SAMPLE SLIDES

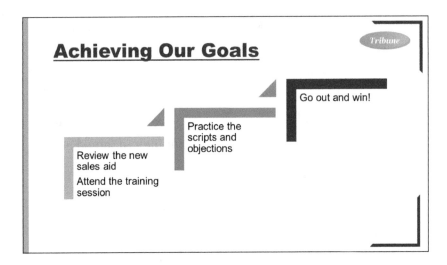

This slide isn't terrible. Cheryl provides actions for the audience members to take. The flow of the diagram indicates rising movement. If she animates this slide, bringing each section in one at a time, it can help convey the steps to take along with a final rallying cry.

However, Cheryl's goal is to inspire her audience, not just give them tasks to complete. A bold slide like this one, with strong imagery and a powerful rhetorical question could help her inspire her team to achieve the company's new goals. It taps into the audience's emotions and offers a challenge. The audience is much more likely to remember this slide than the previous one.

## Chapter 10 Key Takeaways

- Humans learn better from images than text alone. Your slide visuals will play an important part in getting your message across.
- The main types of visuals we use in slide development are images, charts, text, and diagrams.
- Keep in mind the principles of effective communication on slides: relevance, appropriate knowledge, salience, discriminability, compatibility, informative change, and capacity limitation.

# PART 2

# PREPARING TO ENGAGE YOUR AUDIENCE AND ANSWER THEIR QUESTIONS

Giving a presentation is a performance, so let's be sure you're ready. For me, being a working actor taught me invaluable lessons on the subtle aspects of performance and preparation in a business setting. In this part of the book, I'm going to use my experience working as a professional actor to help illustrate the elements of preparation and delivery that you'll need to deliver a smashing presentation. We're also going to explore perhaps the most challenging aspect of presenting—handling audience questions. By borrowing techniques from sales and media training, you'll learn how to maintain composure and provide a response that is on point. Finally, you'll learn how to use your voice and body to strengthen your delivery.

CHAPTER 11

# Commit to Your Preparation

Pressure is a privilege.

—*Billie Jean King*

At this point, you've thought about how to organize and design your presentation so that it resonates with your audience. Now, it's time to make sure it goes seamlessly on the big day. Regardless of how formal your presentation is or how large your audience is, you'll want to consider three factors when you're preparing for your presentation: the setting you'll be presenting in, the technology you'll be using, and the way you practice.

## Your Setting

As an actor, something in your body changes that first day you walk onto the set. Your performance and the stakes at play become more real. You move from a nondistinct rehearsal room to the detailed and perfectly arranged location of the story. This fuels you and helps get you ready to perform. The location of a play is integral to the action. When you watch *West Side Story*, the graffiti, the alleys, and the deserted lots "under the highway" put you in Hell's Kitchen on the west side of Midtown Manhattan. Set and lighting designers work wonders to help the audience—and the actors—feel as though they're in the middle of the action no matter the setting. The same is true when getting ready to present.

You've been drafting your presentation at your desk or in a coffee shop. You've been sketching ideas, developing slides, and walking through your notes. Now, as part of your preparation you need to consider your environment. Where will you be when you give your presentation? Is it a large hall, a conference room, or a customer meeting room? Is it a virtual presentation? How will the room be set up? What are the acoustics like? How will the seating be arranged? All of these are important questions for you, the presenter. The answer to these questions gives you your own "set." Getting comfortable with the location of your presentation before you present will ensure that you will deliver a seamless presentation.

Now, you may not be able to control every aspect of the presentation environment, but it is important to influence what you can, adapt to the elements you can't change, and prepare for the unexpected. We've developed a set of questions that you should know the answers to prior to your presentation. The full set of questions is available on our website, www.talentisvital.com. Some may be obvious, but some may require you to ask your host for details. As a result of your inquiry, you may find that you can change aspects of the setting, such as the lighting or temperature. If you are able, take advantage of the opportunity to create the ideal setting, or as close to ideal as possible. Of course, ideal depends on your communication situation, but if you're presenting in person, here are some guidelines.

## LIGHTING

Lighting should be set so that participants can see handout materials clearly, but the room should not be so bright that the projected slides wash out on the screen. If the room setup permits, you may be able to adjust the lights in different parts of the room. In this instance, you can avoid screen washout by dimming the lights above or near the screen while leaving plenty of light for your audience to read handout materials. You never want the room to be so dark that it puts people to sleep.

## TEMPERATURE

Cool but comfortable is typically better. If the room is too warm, participants tend to become drowsy. If the room is too cold, participants can become distracted or uncomfortable. Avoid extremes on either end. Aim for neither too cold nor too warm.

## ROOM SETUP

Find out how people will be seated at your presentation. The room and setup matter in your ability to see and connect with your audience. Here are some common seating configurations and what you should be thinking about with each:

| SETUP | BENEFITS | CAUTIONS |
|---|---|---|
| U shape | Allows you to move freely Allows you to get close to the audience Allows audience members to see each other | Not good for the audience to interact with each other |
| Classroom Style | Good for lecture-type presentations Good for large audiences who need to write things down | Limits your movement Audience members can't see each other |
| Table Rounds | Great for audience discussion Allows you to move around the room | Some people may need to turn their chairs away from the table |
| Conference Table | Power position Like the U shape, you see everyone, and they see each other | Limits your movement |

## TECHNOLOGY

Unless you're giving a presentation in a small room and have no visual aids, you'll likely be using technology to some degree. For our purposes, we'll include both hardware and software in the technology category. You want to make sure that all the technology needed for your presentation works and works well together. For example, do you have the right connectors to be able to project your presentation? If you have sound or video, do you have adequate speakers? When it comes to technology, whether you're live or virtual, here are a few things you should consider when preparing. You can access a complete **technology preparation checklist** on our website at www. talentisvital.com.

### *Away versus Home*

When presenting in your own office, you know what technology is available and how to troubleshoot technical problems that may arise. At the very least, you know whom to call for help in your office. You also can practice in the setting you'll be giving the presentation. You can and should do a tech "dry run" beforehand. If you're going to present in a location outside your office, however, even if it's just another building on your corporate campus, you need to prepare for more potential problems. Beforehand, you should ask your contact about the room you'll be presenting in using the setup checklist questions we've provided. This may seem like an inconvenience, but it's vital for the success of your presentation. Imagine, after all the hard work you've done in getting ready for your presentation, that you get to the location for your presentation and you're not able to connect your computer to the screen.

## *Video*

If including video in your presentation, you'll want to make sure that you have audio capabilities where you're presenting. Are there speakers? Make sure you're not relying on computer audio only, especially for presentations in larger rooms.

## *Other Technologies*

### Microphone

Will there be a lectern with a microphone? Will there be a microphone that you can move around with? The presence of a microphone will help determine how you can move while presenting as well as how loudly you need to speak to be heard.

### Clicker

A clicker allows you to move more freely around a room while still advancing slides. If you bring your own, make sure the computer you're using has a USB port or is Bluetooth enabled. My favorite clicker is the Logitech Spotlight Presentation Remote. The device and software combination allows you to do all the basics like advancing and blacking out slides, but it also allows you to use the pointer on a TV monitor—something that is important now that most conference rooms no longer use projectors. It also has a spotlight feature that allows you to focus on an area of the slide while dimming other areas.

## *A Backup Plan*

Because technology can be unreliable, I like to have a backup plan that includes several levels of contingency planning. First, I always have a hard copy of my presentation and my notes—no matter what. I even have a printed copy in front of me when I present virtually. Next, I make sure I have a copy of my presentation on a portable storage device. Digital storage is inexpensive. Even an image-heavy presentation with video can fit on a thumb drive. Finally, I always have my presentation backed up in the cloud so I can access it from anywhere if necessary. It always feels good to have the presentation in multiple locations, even if you never need to access it there.

> **Good preparation is one of the most important things you can do to combat prepresentation nerves.**

When it comes to backup plans, one question I always ask myself is "If I had to give this presentation with no slides, no notes, and no handouts, could I do it?" Knowing your topic and knowing your presentation is the best backup plan you can have. The key to this is intentional practice, something that we in the theater call rehearsal. When you know how to practice, you'll be able to give your presentation anytime, anywhere.

### Practice

Practice is a cornerstone of performance but one that many presenters don't always devote enough time to doing. If you neglect to practice, you know the consequences. No one likes being in front of a group of people and not feeling prepared. In fact, as we discussed earlier, good preparation is one of the most important things you can do to combat prepresentation nerves. So how should you practice?

Just as rehearsing a play is more than memorizing and reciting lines, preparing for your presentation is more than just reading your slides out loud. Actors prepare by knowing what they're doing at every moment they are on stage. They do this by breaking their script into beats, the smallest unit of action in a play. A beat is also the time it takes a character to play out a single intention in pursuit of their objective. Fortunately, if you've created a good structure and you've organized your slides as we've discussed, your beats are already created for you. Every slide is a beat, and every beat has an objective. In practicing for your presentation, you should think critically about what your objective is for every slide, and then think about what you need to do to accomplish it. Go back to your Know-Feel-Do Matrix. Where are you trying to get your audience to throughout your presentation? What strategies will you employ in getting them there? It all comes down to actions you can take. Here are a few, for example:

- Welcome the audience.
- Describe the problem.
- Emphasize a point.
- Ask a question.
- Present the evidence.
- Tell a story.
- Surprise the audience.

These are all verbs—action words. They are things you can do. Then, when you deliver your presentation, it's your objectives you're focused on accomplishing and not how you look, or sound, or what you do with your hands. They help you avoid being self-conscious. They keep you in the moment because you're *doing* something. I recommend this: take your index cards out, and write your objective on the bottom of the front where you have your headline and the image that will be on the slide. Remember that on the back side you'll have your talking points, stories, or anecdotes that go along with that slide.

### Learn Your Flow

Actors learn lines, and presenters learn flow. That's why we put so much emphasis on it when we discussed building your presentation.

127

Concentrate on the headlines, and make sure you can list them in order. Once you feel comfortable with the flow, you can start to focus on the supporting ideas and evidence for each of the major points you'll make.

### Rehearse Out Loud

There is no substitute for saying the words out loud. Mental rehearsal is important, and it's more convenient than rehearsing out loud. After all, no one on the airplane wants to hear your presentation, but you need to find time to practice out loud and hear yourself say the words. The most important benefit of rehearsing out loud is that when it's time to present, you will naturally signal to the audience, "Hey, I've done this before." You'll have increased confidence, and that will help put you and your audience at ease.

### Record Yourself

While you're rehearsing, go ahead and record yourself speaking the presentation. In fact, take a video of yourself. This is a great way to practice your presentation because it gives you the immediate feedback you need to adjust your delivery to have the most impact. With the technology in your pocket, you have everything you need to get critical visual and auditory feedback in the moment.

All smartphones have a voice recorder and video camera. This is the simplest way to record yourself. You can run your slides on your computer, have your notes in front of you, turn your phone's voice recorder on, and you're all set. When you listen back, listen for the following things:

- **Your pace:** Does it sound conversational? Is it too fast for the audience to follow and comprehend you? Is it too slow and laborious?

- **Your vocal variety:** Are you creating vocal interest and energy by varying your pitch, rate, and volume?
- **Verbal fillers:** Is your presentation filled with *ums, ahs, likes,* and *sos?*
- **Logic and flow:** Does the work you did in creating structure transfer to the spoken word? Will the audience be able to easily follow your logic?

If you're using video, add these items to the things you're looking for:

- Do you look relaxed? Is there tension in your shoulders and neck?
- Do you come to life while presenting? Are your facial expressions adding to your communication?
- Are you moving too much? Rocking? Pacing?

# Use PowerPoint Speaker Coach or Other Artificial Intelligence Tools

The technology in your pocket is getting better and better all the time. I want to spend a little time talking about one of these innovations that can help you become a better presenter: Microsoft's Speaker Coach. This program uses artificial intelligence that listens to your presentation rehearsal and creates a comprehensive feedback report.

## HOW SPEAKER COACH WORKS

Speaker Coach is a feature in Microsoft 365 and is as easy to access as any of PowerPoint's other ribbon features. In the Slide Show tab, click on Rehearse with Coach, and then click the Start Rehearsing button in the bottom-right corner. Speaker Coach will use your computer's microphone to "hear" your speech. If it detects filler words, sensitive language, or vocal rates or pitches that are too high or too low, it'll give you an onscreen reminder so you can adjust your delivery. Once you're done, Speaker Coach provides a report that is divided into six sections: "Summary," "Originality," "Sensitive Phrases," "Pace," "Pitch," and "Fillers." While there's much more to strong delivery than what's covered in these sections, Speaker Coach can still help you fine-tune some of the most crucial elements of a presentation.

## Dealing with Anxiety

As the presentation date gets closer and you start to intensify your rehearsal, you may experience some anxiety. In fact, of all the things my clients ask for help with, dealing with their preperformance nerves is the one I get the most. It's also the request that concerns me the most, and that is for a couple of reasons. First, when someone has worked hard on their talk, it's tough to see them worry so much about it that they don't look forward to delivering it. The second reason is that speaker anxiety gets in the way of communicating your message clearly and coherently.

It's important to differentiate between healthy nervous excitement and speaker anxiety. When we're preparing for a high-stakes presentation, our brain sends us a signal that says, "Get ready! Take this seriously! This is important!" This type of signal is constructive—it reminds us that we need to pay attention and do the preparation. Speaker anxiety, on the other hand, is different. It can be all consuming, leading to lost sleep and even to looking for ways to avoid or cancel presentations. Feeling uneasy, fearful, and nervous before presenting is a common experience. In fact, many exceptional speakers, including Winston Churchill, John F. Kennedy, Margaret Thatcher, and Barbra Streisand, have all reported they experienced anxiety and nervousness about speaking in public. Research shows that being anxious about public speaking does not discriminate. Anyone can experience it, and those who do dread presenting to the point that they avoid it whenever possible. This is problematic for business professionals, because if you avoid giving public presentations, it will likely keep you from advancing in your career.

My own encounter with a bout of speaker anxiety made me keenly interested in the psychology and physiology of communication apprehension—one part of public speaking anxiety. By examining my own experience, I learned just how unpredictable and elusive it can be. For as long as I can remember, I wanted to be an actor. As a wide-eyed freshman in high school, I joined the drama club. From the first moment I stepped on stage until my midfifties, I never experienced speaking anxiety. Granted, I had a healthy dose of preperformance nerves and jitters. But I never experienced anxiety or panic.

All that changed one evening in a hotel room in Phoenix. I was getting ready for a training presentation I would give the next day, and I began to feel my palms sweat. My heart was racing. I was experiencing all the symptoms of a full-on panic attack. The last thing I wanted to do was give that presentation the next day. That night, I couldn't sleep, and thoughts of dread haunted me as I tossed and turned. In that moment, my brain was telling me that dying would have been better than getting up to speak. Maybe that's why people say they fear public speaking more than death.

Thankfully, my wife talked me off the ledge. With her words and God's grace, I made it through that presentation, but to my surprise, it happened several more times over the next few months. I decided I needed to do something about it. Presenting was my livelihood, so I had to understand what was going on. I sought counseling and dived into the psychology of speaker anxiety. I decided that if I could ever get my joy of speaking back, I'd make sure I'd help as many people as I could overcome their own fears. Here are some of the most important things I learned.

## WHY YOU GET ANXIOUS ABOUT SPEAKING
### *You Don't Think You're Good at Public Speaking*

Sometimes we become anxious because we don't believe we have the skill to accomplish the task. I wouldn't want to jump out of an airplane or drive a motorcycle without the skill required to survive. If you don't have any training or practice in giving high-stakes presentations, I don't blame you for being nervous! But you can learn. In fact, you already know more than you did when you first picked up this book!

### *Learned Responses*

Sometimes we are at the mercy of our own past learned responses—that is, at least until we're aware of them. For example, if you received praise and positive reinforcement for speaking, you would associate positive consequences with communication. On the contrary, if you received harsh criticism or if people made fun of you when you spoke, you will associate speaking with negative consequences. Likewise, if you observed your parents or others around you exhibiting fear of speaking, you may have learned to be cautious yourself because it appeared to be a dangerous situation. It takes work, and sometimes a good counselor, to help with deeply ingrained response patterns. But if you need to speak publicly as part of your profession, the tips in the next section can help. They won't replace the benefits of counseling, but they will give you something concrete to work on.

### *Worrisome Thoughts*

Worrisome thoughts are sometimes called negative self-talk or irrational thinking. This is your mind trying to help you escape what you see as a threat. If it can convince you that you'll fail or experience some danger, you won't do it. Isn't it kind of your mind to be so helpful?

### *Overactivation of Body Chemistry*

This category sounds so clinical, but everyone experiences it. I'm sure you can recall a time when you saw a car fly through an intersection and you had to slam on the brakes. At that moment, without your conscious help, a flood of chemicals like adrenaline and cortisol released in your body. They helped you focus and respond appropriately to the situation while also temporarily shutting down other functions like rational thinking and hunger. That's why if you are anxious before you speak, chances are you don't feel like sitting down for a big meal. While those chemicals are great if you need to get out of the way of a speeding car, they can hamper your ability to deliver a great presentation.

### *Performance Orientation*

Another reason that anxiety creeps up on us when we're getting ready to speak in public is too much focus on the outcome or consequences of what you're doing. In other words, you are worried about the social implications, like your status or how you are perceived by the audience. This is also a result of a performance orientation. Throughout this book we've been talking about presenting as a kind of performance. Let's take a moment to differentiate a healthy performance mindset from one that is unhealthy and causes stress.

An unhealthy performance mindset is when you put the focus on yourself. You think, *What will they think of me? How do I look? How do I sound? How will I be remembered?* A healthy performance mindset is when you put your focus on the objective that you set out to achieve and what your audience will experience and learn. Getting the focus off yourself and onto the audience and your objective will change the way you look at presenting and performing any difficult task. Yes, presenting is a performance, but how we understand performance makes all the difference in *how* we perform.

As I noted in the introduction, one of the most enjoyable and satisfying things about presenting is that it's live. You are meeting, talking to, and sharing ideas with other people in real time. I understand that there are often high stakes when presenting. When we recognize that, our mind wants to prepare us. It calls out for our attention and signals that we need to get ready. Kept in perspective, that is a great service to us. Thank you, brain! To keep it in perspective, however, we need to remember that the interaction with others in a live setting provides the opportunity to move something forward, create something, solve a problem, or change something for the better. It's still difficult to manage those nerves even when you try to keep these things in mind.

> **Put your focus on the objective that you set out to achieve and what your audience will experience and learn.**

I wish there were a way to wave a magic wand and make every one of my students' nerves go away—especially the ones who really struggle. Heck, I wish I could do it for myself! But I can't. What I can offer are some techniques that can help you get closer to *presentation peace*—the place where you can worry less and look forward to your presentations. But it takes consistent practice. There are many techniques for dealing with speaker anxiety. We won't be able to cover them all, but here are some practical, concrete, and repeatable techniques for dealing with how our mind and body respond when we are getting ready to present.

## *Attacking Speaker Anxiety*

I've organized a few techniques for tackling speaker anxiety for you here. In my experience, I've found that there are things you can do with your body to calm yourself and others that address the chaos in your mind. I've also separated them by those that can be used when the nerves hit just before speaking in the moment and those that are longer-term solutions for addressing speech apprehension.

## *For Your Mind, in the Moment*

### Put the Rational-Thinking Part of Your Mind to Work

When we feel threatened, our amazing brains get us ready for fight or flight. Blood moves to our muscles and extremities, and the rational-thinking part of our brain takes a back seat. When a threat is imminent, like another car speeding toward yours at seventy miles an hour, your brain doesn't want you thinking about the physics of the impact. It wants you to get the hell out of the way as fast as possible. While a presentation can feel like an impending crash, however, it isn't. When you feel that cortisol kicking in, you've got to get your brain back to thinking rationally. One way to do that is to call on the part of your brain that controls rational thinking. You can do it by giving it a rational-thinking task—something you know backward and forward. This can be multiplication tables or counting backward by threes or sixes. It sounds silly, but it helps manage the lizard part of our brain that can take over at the wrong time.

### Let Your Breath Calm You

The best breathing exercise I've come across, and one I practice regularly, is called the Relaxing Breath. I learned this one from Dr. Andrew Weil, a holistic medical practitioner who has a great program on breathing. The way it works is to take a four-count inhale through your nose, hold for a count of seven, and then exhale, as if you were breathing through a straw, for a count of eight. Note that the exhale is twice as long as the inhale. This complete exhale allows you to get rid of all the stale air in your lungs and readies them for a nice, full, deep inhale to follow. Breathing out through pursed lips also helps you develop control over the movement of the diaphragm and abdominal muscles. It's a great breathing technique for when you are feeling nervous. The holding of the breath and the long exhale really help relax you. I recommend doing these two or three times before a presentation. Careful not to do too much—you don't want to hyperventilate! And you don't need to purse your lips when you're in public. You can just exhale slowly and with control—and no one will know that you're taking a moment for yourself.

### Take a Meditation Moment

Before a high-stakes presentation, our minds race. *What if I forget what to say? What if they don't like me? What if? What if? What if?* These are all projections, and they come hard and fast. They throw you off balance with the frenetic noise bouncing around in your head. A distracted and confused mind does not allow for peak performance. What you need to do is get quiet and get focused. You can do this with a meditation moment.

A meditation moment is when you consciously put all your focus on something concrete outside of your mind, like your breathing rhythm, an object, or the background noise in a room. Jeff Warren from Calm, a mindfulness company, calls this a home base. Find a quiet spot. Sit up straight, and relax your shoulders. Close your eyes, and exhale all the stale air out of your lungs. Begin to breathe slowly and rhythmically, inhaling and exhaling through your nose. Put your attention on something concrete, like the air moving in and out of your nose or a background sound, like the sound of distant traffic or air blowing through a vent. Anything that moves your focus onto something other than your racing thoughts. You may find yourself coming back to your thoughts periodically. That's okay; just keep going back to your home base—the breath or the sound. After even just a minute of this solid concentration, you will find yourself relaxing. This is the foundation of meditation, and it's a great long-term practice as well. Check out our website for some great sources for developing a meditation practice.

**Find Your Flow**

Finding your flow is about what top performers call being in the zone. Flow theory was developed by psychologist Mihaly Csikszentmihalyi. At its essence, flow is a state of consciousness where you become totally absorbed in what you are doing to the exclusion of all other thoughts and emotions. It's about focus. Giving a presentation, like playing a sport or chess, provides a special opportunity to make flow happen. Getting into flow—or the zone, as it is often called—requires that you learn to focus your attention on what you are doing and not on the outcome. World-class performers know that to achieve a flow state, they must do a few important things:

- **Be Totally Absorbed in What You Are Doing**

  In my acting training, we learned what it feels like to be totally absorbed in a task. Our acting teacher spilled a saltshaker all over a table onstage and then asked us each to count each individual salt crystal. We had to *really* count them for what seemed like an eternity. The activity required a great deal of focus, but it helped us learn how to concentrate intensely. When you can find that level of focus in your own presentation, you'll find that not only does your anxiety decrease but you also draw your audience's focus to you. Think back to my Rubik's cube example. Find that focus in your presentation, and you'll see how everything else just falls away.

- **Keep Your Objective Front and Center**
  Another thing you must focus on to give a successful presentation is the goal that you created. It's so important when presenting to constantly remind yourself of your objective. It keeps you moving forward and helps you avoid self-consciousness.

- **Use Visualization and Mental Rehearsal**
  Many performers use a technique called creative visualization to help them focus and find flow. Creative visualization is a cognitive process where you purposely generate a mental image of the desired performance ahead of time. It's a technique used to help you stay focused and reduce stress. It's a form of mental rehearsal where you see yourself achieving your ideal objective. You see, when you can imagine your best performance in your mind, you trick your brain into relaxing and doing exactly that—giving a great presentation.

  When using visualization, you should try to imagine an outcome that is as specific as possible. Try to see things in your mind that are concrete, like the clothes you're wearing, the location of the screen, and the way you move around the room. The more detail you use, the easier it is to immerse yourself in the visualization.

- **Have a Routine**
  If you build a great routine when you're not performing, it will come much easier when you are. For example, if you develop a warm-up routine and do it every day, you'll be able

to execute your routine easily on the day of your presentation despite your prepresentation nerves. The routine will calm and focus you. Your mind will recognize that you've been there before. It's another way to get back to that home base I mentioned before.

### *Dealing with How Your Body Feels*

Let's talk about some ways to address how apprehension and fear affect your body. Earlier, we talked about fight or flight. When we feel threatened, our glands secrete adrenaline and cortisol to get us ready to get out of the way of that car or fight that large woolly mammoth. I find that these hormones produce two different feelings in my body. One sensation is tension. Our bodies can get rigid and tense in these moments, so we need to work on relaxing them. To do so, try progressive muscle relaxation.

Progressive muscle relaxation is a technique where you monitor the tension in a specific muscle group by first tensing and then relaxing the muscle. You can start from the top of your body (your head) or the bottom of your body (your feet). Bring your attention to that area. For the purposes of our example, let's start with the feet. Tense one foot for ten seconds, and then release the muscle. Allow yourself to feel the blood flow into that relaxed muscle. Now, move to the other foot. As you progress, move your attention up your body—from your feet to your ankles, your ankles to your calves, your calves to your thighs. Continue to move your focus up your body until you reach the top of your head. You should feel more relaxed. If you don't, start over. Or start from your head and work down to your feet. This is a great technique to use several times during the day prior to your presentation. It is simple and helps avoid muscle tension that when unaddressed can negatively impact your performance.

The other way you may feel before a presentation is amped up from all the adrenaline pumping through your body. Add coffee to the chemicals swimming in your bloodstream, and you'll feel like you're ready to be shot to the moon! Fighting the adrenaline with some exercise-induced endorphins can be very helpful. Any way to physically expel that extra energy will be key. Try out some jumping jacks! And if you're not physically able to do strenuous exercise, I find that shaking your hands and feet vigorously for fifteen to thirty seconds also helps.

Exercise is good for both long-term health and preperformance prep. Presenting is a physical activity, so you need to get your body ready. We all know the long-term benefits of regular exercise, but there are some great short-term benefits as a well—especially for presenters. In one study, researchers found that participants who completed fifteen minutes of moderate-intensity stationary cycling had faster reaction times on working memory tasks immediately after the exercise.[5] That can come in very handy for that postpresentation question-and-answer session. Try to plan time for a physical activity prior to your presentation. It can be a brisk walk if you're at the office, or do some squats, push-ups, and sit-ups before you leave the house.

---

5    C. L. Hogan, J. Mata, and L. L Carstensen, "Exercise Holds Immediate Benefits for Affect and Cognition in Younger and Older Adults," *Psychology and Aging* 28, no. 2 (2013): 587–594, https://doi.org/10.1037/a0032634.

# Chapter 11 Key Takeaways

- Preparation is critical for a successful performance. There are three things you should be focused on in your preparation: your setting, your technology, and your practice.
- Use the setting and technology checklists to eliminate any last-minute issues that will distract you from peak performance.
- Develop a rehearsal routine that works for you, and commit to it.
- It's normal to feel nervous before a high-stakes presentation. Manage your breath and self-talk to help quiet your mind and get focused.

# CHAPTER 12

# Strengthen Your Delivery

Of all the talents bestowed upon men, none is so
precious as the gift of oratory. He who enjoys it wields
a power more durable than that of a great king.

—*Winston Churchill*

In our workshops, I ask participants to list the attributes of a great presenter. They usually say that they look and sound comfortable. They're passionate and exude confidence. They make eye contact. They relate to the audience. A great presenter, in their words, is natural. Only a select few say that a great presenter is logical or that they present convincing supporting evidence. Why is that? We know now that good presenters need to use logic and must support their claims with evidence, but audiences respond most directly to *how* someone delivers their presentation. Presenting is a physical activity. Your voice and body are the instruments you will use to "play" your presentation. Just like any good musician learns the intricacies of what their instrument can do, you must learn how to use these tools to communicate.

Great presenters understand how to use their voice and body to enhance their message and achieve their communication objective. The goal is to be in complete control of these physical aspects of communication. When you are, you will be relaxed and centered before and during every presentation. The tips and techniques that I'll share with you will help you tune your instrument. They will help you stay relaxed, fully present, and in command of the stage, wherever that may be for you.

Here's an important note about the techniques we'll cover in this chapter. You should think consciously about them during practice and rehearsal but not while you are presenting. For example, I'm going to teach you about using gestures, but I don't want you thinking about your hands when you're presenting. That's when you should be focused solely on your objective. The work we do in this chapter will help you build skills during practice and rehearsal. When it comes time for your presentation, you will have already incorporated them, and they will come naturally.

## Your Body Speaks

One of my favorite expressions is "You can't not communicate." Everything you do or don't do sends a message. There's been plenty of research to support just how much nonverbal communication matters. In his book *Power Cues: The Subtle Science of Leading Groups, Persuading Others, and Maximizing Your Personal Impact*, author Nick Morgan explores how things like posture, eye contact, arm positions, or the way you sit make a difference in the overall impression you make on your audience and ultimately how they'll respond to your message.

Learning to move your body easily and fluidly helps you look and feel confident, and it will help you develop your speaking voice as well. When participants in our workshops watch themselves on video, they often say they look wooden or stiff. That lack of relaxation is often caused by fear. Or it's the result of being too self-conscious. As we discussed earlier, their fight-or-flight responses are causing them to freeze up. They think, *Everyone is looking at me. What should I do with my hands or arms?* Once you start thinking about yourself while you're presenting, you're sunk.

Your movement during a presentation will vary based on where you're presenting. Chuck will be at a conference table in a small room. He's likely to stay seated for his entire presentation, but Cheryl will be on a large stage at her company meeting. And while they are both in different settings, they both need to be relaxed and centered from the moment they are called upon to speak until they have returned to their seats.

> **Learning to move your body easily and fluidly helps you look and feel confident.**

In our classroom training workshops, we practice "taking the stage." We use a formal presentation setting, and everyone gets a chance to present their work. I call each person by name and provide a brief introduction, after which they stand, walk to the front of the room, and begin their presentation. To some, it seems silly and almost overkill. But the participants quickly realize the amount of self-consciousness they feel and demonstrate through their body language. When they review the video of their introduction, they see themselves shifting side to side or freezing up into rigid facial expression.

The tips and techniques I'll give you for good physical presence will help relax you and make you feel more confident. But it's not just about putting yourself at ease. When you take the stage of your presentation in a relaxed and confident manner, you put the audience at ease too. They immediately feel like they are in good hands. This helps reduce the uncertainty any audience feels when they are watching a live performance. You'll also want to make an immediate connection with them. This reassures them and shows that you're paying attention to them, even subconsciously. Calmly walking to the front of the room, making eye contact, and having a relaxed, pleasant face can help put the audience at ease.

From the moment your name is called, your audience is watching and taking in everything you do. If you walk timidly to the front of the room, the audience sees that and interprets it as fear. They will become uncomfortable, and you will lose some of the credibility that we know matters so much. But if you move with purpose and intentionality, it sends a very different message, and it builds excitement and anticipation. Here are the elements of physical presence on the platform that you need to master.

## POSTURE

Maya Angelou said, "Stand up straight and realize who you are, that you tower over your circumstances." Let's face it, people associate a strong and upright posture with winners. Just look at the animal kingdom and how animals communicate strength. They expand. Think of a peacock extending its feathers or a bear standing up on its hind legs. "Expanding your body frees you to approach, act, and persist," notes Amy Cuddy, a Harvard Business School professor and author of *Presence*. A strong and upright posture is always important when presenting—even if you're sitting down.

But there's more to posture than just standing up straight. The goal is to be relaxed, grounded, confident, and poised. That means being ready to adapt your physical presence to whatever you need. The ability to do this comes from you being in a state of balance. While there are many benefits to the power posing that Professor Cuddy discusses in her book, I advocate having poise over power. Here's a simple activity to help you develop a strong, comfortable, and balanced posture.

146

Stand with your feet shoulder-width apart, rise up on your tiptoes, and hold for three seconds. Now, imagine the top of your head staying right where it is while you lower your heels. It will feel like you are being stretched from the top of your head to the bottoms of your feet. Try to keep that feeling of elongation when you are presenting. Like anything, don't overdo it. You'll look stiff and unnatural. Try to find the balance between extension and relaxation. Remember, if you practice this in advance and make good posture a habit, you won't need to think about it when you're presenting.

## OPENNESS

Openness signals confidence. It indicates that you are prepared and comfortable with your message. Even if you have the normal nerves that go with performing, you want to stay open to your audience. What does that mean? Well, here's a simple exercise to get you used to being available to your audience. Imagine your audience in front of you, face them in your mind, and allow your arms to spread out. Don't lock your elbows to your sides—try to raise your arms in a relaxed and open way. Take a deep breath and, in your mind, invite the audience in. Remember this open feeling when you are presenting, and keep your whole body available to your audience as you give your presentation.

> **Eye contact is not just looking at the audience. It's about connecting with them.**

### *Eye Contact*

Eye contact is not just looking at the audience. It's about connecting with them. Eye contact communicates that you are present, not just for the whole room but for that specific person with whom you're making eye contact. If actors in a scene aren't making eye contact with each other, the audience can spot it a mile away. And if you, as a presenter, aren't making true eye contact with your audience, they know that too. Though you may not be able to make direct eye contact with every member of a large audience, if you make genuine eye contact with some members of the audience, the rest of the audience will feel it. All good presenters are other oriented. Now, we've been talking about the audience since chapter 1. We do audience analysis and understand what's in it for them so that we can deliver a great presentation. Audience centrality is at the heart of developing and delivering a successful presentation.

The idea of being other oriented is how actors learn to be less self-conscious and more present and alive. When I was in acting school, we worked endlessly on an activity called repetition. This activity was simple. You would look at the other person that you were working with and find something that was truthful about them. Maybe they were wearing a blue shirt, so you would start and say, "You're wearing a blue shirt." Then your partner would repeat exactly what you said so there was a continuous dialogue with a simple script: "You're wearing a blue shirt." Now, there were many reasons for this activity, but the main goal was to help the actor be less self-conscious. You do that by putting your attention on the other person. You listen and focus on the other actor. Make genuine eye contact with the audience. They'll feel it.

### *Movement*

When actors are rehearsing a play, in addition to working on their character and memorizing their lines, they are also working on blocking, or the movement of the characters on the stage. How they enter and exit, how they move when other characters enter, and how they use props—these movements all provide a sense of realism to the scene. When it all comes together, the audience sees what looks natural and like real life. But the actors have carefully planned out every move onstage. Movement in a presentation won't be as complex as the choreography of a play, but careful attention to a few aspects of movement will help you move fluidly and will enhance the experience for your audience.

Movement creates energy and makes your presentation more interesting and engaging. You must move with purpose. You must have a reason for moving. Maybe it's to point out a chart or speak directly to a segment of the audience. Maybe it's to create a sense of intimacy by moving closer to them. Keep in mind that our eyes are always scanning for movement. It's an ancient and unconscious means of self-preservation. If you're resting peacefully, you will snap to attention when you see movement that could threaten you. Remember that when you want to make a key point or get the audience's attention. If you move with purpose, the audience will instinctively follow you and tune in.

## When You're Standing

Movement is important, but it should start from a balanced and stable neutral position. You must find that neutral starting point, and here's how:

- Keep your weight evenly distributed between your two feet.
- Keep your feet pointed toward your audience.
- Allow your arms to drop freely from your shoulders.
- Imagine a string lifting you up from the top of your head and one pulling the base of your spine down.
- Allow your head to stay relaxed so you can turn either way simply and easily.

## When You're Seated

In most office or conference room settings, you won't need to move much—first, because the presentation probably doesn't call for it, and second, there usually isn't that much space. Let's talk about a few things you should do when you are seated for a presentation:

- Sit forward on the edge of your chair.
- Plant both feet on the floor.
- Don't swivel or rock in the chair.
- Sit up straight.
- Keep your hands and arms on the table.

## Your Hands

I'm not going to tell you how to move your hands. They will move naturally and freely when you are relaxed, focused, and confident. There are a few things, however, that you should keep in mind about your hands while rehearsing:

- Be careful not to indicate aggression with your hands. Never point at the audience. If you need to indicate something in the direction of the audience, use an open hand—that is, your palm facing up and fingers relaxed.
- Allow your elbows to move away from your body.
- If you are using a lectern, keep your hands relaxed—don't clutch the lectern. Remember, you want your hands free to move. It's especially important to gesture if you're using a lectern, as the rest of you won't be moving.

# Working with Your Visual Aids

For most of your business presentations, you'll be using slides or a flip chart as your visual aids. If you are standing, the way you position yourself to show the visual aids will be important. The goal is to continue to face the audience while referring them to the visuals. This means staying in an open position with the screen next to you.

One of the hot topics during the feedback sections of our workshops is reading from the slides. There is a tendency among inexperienced presenters to look at the slide and read the content. Sometimes the need for safety is so strong that presenters just can't resist the lifeline. I'm sure we've all been in presentations where this has happened. When it does, the audience and presenter are no longer connected because the speaker is paying more attention to the screen than to the audience. The better you know the material and the better rehearsed you are, the less pull you will feel to look at the slides, other than as a brief orientation. Keep in mind that this is not just a problem with presenting—it's also a design problem. If there are a lot of words on a slide, it's easy to get sucked into reading them. In previous chapters, we discussed the importance of designing slides that are visually appealing, convey meaning, and use words strategically, not as speaker notes. With that said, it's often impossible to commit an entire presentation to memory. While slides should not be your speaker notes, they can act as prompts. Here are a few tips for working with your visual aids.

When presenting in person, ensure you are properly placed in relationship to the screen where you are projecting your slides. You don't want to stand right in front of it where you are blocking the content or too far out of the field of view where the audience can't see you and the screen together. Also, if you stand too far in front of the screen, when you do need to refer to something on the slide, you'll have to turn your back to the audience. This is a no-no. It's better to stand closer or in the same plane as the screen when you're referring to anything in your visual aids.

Think about the transition from one slide to the next. This should not be difficult if you worked on your transitions when drafting your content. How does the story move from slide to slide? And how will you help the audience follow the story? For example, you can make a closure statement on one slide, something like, "From this timeline, you can see that we've offered an option for an accelerated launch date." And then pair it with a simple transition statement to help the audience follow the story: "There are some cost implications of that approach, so let's take a look at that now."

Because we all respond reflexively to movement, an audience's eyes will immediately move to the title or to the most prominent visual on the slide as soon as you advance to the next one. The first thing to do is briefly pause. Allow the audience a moment to orient to the new slide. If you don't, whatever you say may be lost. During this time, it is okay to briefly look at the screen to orient yourself and get a quick refresher of what the discussion will be.

After the audience has had a moment to look, you can begin to tell the story on this slide. A well-designed slide will prepare the audience in two ways. The headline and the visual should encapsulate the essence of the message—what's important. Your job is to *add value* to what's on the slide. You do that by describing, interpreting, analyzing, or discussing the information on the slide to support your argument and achieve your objective.

Keep in mind that your audience has not seen your slides or may not be as familiar with the material as you. You'll need to help direct their visual focus. This is especially important when you are using data visualizations. For example, if you're using a bar chart, you should orient the audience to the X axis, then the Y axis, and then any color or shape information that will help them better understand the visual. Remember that all charts are a means of showing a relationship in the data. Don't be afraid to verbalize just what the relationship is and why it's important.

## YOUR VOICE

Think about a monologue that you love from a play or movie, or a sermon that moved you, or a famous speech, like Martin Luther King Jr.'s "I Have a Dream" speech. I'm sure that when you listened, you were not thinking about the volume, the rate of speech, or the speaker's articulation and enunciation. That's because the speaker captured your attention, and you were engulfed in the experience. Great presenters and speakers know how to use their voice to great effect. They use it to convey energy and passion. They convey rich emotion or a sense of urgency. They convey trust and confidence. And just as actors rehearse their lines aloud using their voice to help convey their intention, you too must practice the basics of vocal production in your own rehearsal. This way, when you are on the platform on the day, neither you nor your audience is consciously thinking about your voice. Instead, you're both engaged in your message and the emotion you are conveying.

When presenters fail to engage their audiences with their voice, here's the type of feedback they usually get:

- They lack the ability to project and fill the room. The audience can't hear them.
- They're speaking too fast or too slow.
- They sound nervous.
- They speak with an annoying downward or upward inflection pattern.

- They're monotone with no variety in their pitch.
- They sound stilted or stiff.
- They use too many verbal fillers.

I'm going to give you some tips and techniques to avoid these pitfalls, the goal of which is to help you develop vocal energy. I want your voice to be ready to convey your message, express emotion, and capture the attention of your audience. Getting your voice ready in rehearsal will make it that much easier to do so when you need to present.

My favorite story of overcoming difficulties with speech is about Demosthenes. He lived in Greece in about 350 BC. In ancient Greek society, citizens were expected to be able to speak publicly in court to resolve disputes and in political debates in the public square. When Demosthenes was eighteen, he was cheated out of his inheritance by his guardians, and he wanted to get it back. To do so, he had to go to the public court and make his argument orally. The problem was, Demosthenes did not have a strong physical presence. He spent most of his time reading Thucydides, not working out at the gymnasium. Further compromising his presentation skills, he also had a speech impediment. According to Plutarch, he had a "perplexed and indistinct utterance and a shortness of breath, which ... much obscured the sense and meaning of what he spoke." Still, he was determined to succeed. He created his own development plan to make himself a better presenter—just like you!

The legend goes that he found a cave near the Aegean Sea as his rehearsal spot. There, he practiced his projection so that he could be heard over the roaring of the waves. He filled his mouth with pebbles to help him strengthen his articulators—his tongue, jaw, lips, and palate. To help develop his breath, he ran up and down hills and along the shore reciting those same speeches until he could do it without running out of breath. Every day, he recited the works of Thucydides to warm up and ended the day by rehearsing his argument against his guardians. And his plan worked! He returned to Athens, won his case, and went on to become one of the most admired and accomplished public speakers in ancient Greece.

If you're looking for a more modern example of persistence and practice in developing your voice, watch *The King's Speech*. In this 2010 film, Geoffrey Rush plays Lionel Logue, an eccentric but passionately committed speech teacher in 1940s London. He is hired to help King George V (played by Colin Firth) overcome his stutter and fear of speaking in public as he prepares to address the British people on the eve of World War II. If you've ever worried about speaking in public, you will relate to the reluctant king.

These stories have always inspired me. They may be the best examples of overcoming challenges with presenting in public. If you're looking to improve your platform skills, keep Demosthenes and King George V in mind as you work through these exercises.

## LEARNING TO USE YOUR BREATH

All voice work starts with the breath. That's because the voice is supported by the breath, and it rides on the breath. Your breath is controlled by your diaphragm, the large muscle at the bottom of your rib cage that separates the lungs from the abdominal cavity. The diaphragm expands and contracts and allows you to inhale and exhale. When you inhale, the diaphragm moves down, allowing air to fill the lungs. When you exhale, the diaphragm relaxes and moves up, helping you expel air from your lungs. Your body instinctively knows how to breathe with the greatest efficiency. In fact, you probably do your best breathing while you're sleeping. Your abdominal muscles and your diaphragm are relaxed, and your breathing is even and effortless. That's just what you want to feel when you're speaking.

Unfortunately, most of us carry around a lot of tension during a busy workday. And that tension gets exacerbated when we give an important presentation. All that tension makes breathing deeply and easily much harder, but to make good sound, you need steady and even breathing. See the dilemma? How do you keep your breath smooth and even when you're nervous? I'm sure it's not going to surprise you that it comes down to practice. We need to train our breathing muscles to relax, and we need to do that work in advance of our presentation. That's one of the reasons these next few exercises will help you. They're practice exercises that you can do anytime to improve your breath control, but they also have an added benefit. They can be a "just in time" first aid kit for prepresentation nerves. Here are my favorites:

## *The 4–7–8 Relaxing Breath*

In previous chapters, I covered 4–7–8 breath, but it bears repeating here. The way it works is to take a four-count inhale through your nose, hold for a count of seven, and then exhale, as if you were breathing through a straw, for a count of eight. You'll notice that the exhale is twice as long as the inhale. This complete exhale allows you to get rid of all the stale air in your lungs and allows for a nice, full, deep inhale to follow. Breathing out through pursed lips helps you develop control over the movement of the diaphragm and abdominal muscles.

This is also a great breathing technique if you are feeling nervous. The holding of the breath and the long exhale really help relax you. I recommend doing these two or three times before a presentation, but be careful not to do too much—you don't want to hyperventilate! And don't worry, you don't need to purse your lips when you're in public—you can just exhale slowly and with control.

## *Make the Candle Flicker*

Here's another great exercise to help you build breath control and support. In this exercise you're going to make a candle flame flicker. I suggest doing this with a real candle at first, and then you can transition to an imaginary candle so you can take this exercise on the road. Let's start with a real candle. Light the candle, and hold it about an arm's distance way. Then inhale for a count of four, and blow out for a count of four. Try to make the flame flicker, but be careful not to blow the candle out. This will help you control your exhale and regulate your breath on command.

After you've done several sets using a count of four, increase your inhale/exhale count to five, and so on until you reach ten. Once you've mastered this activity using the real candle, you can try it using an imaginary candle. This is a great breathing workout.

## *Straw Breathing*

For this next exercise, you're going to need a few props, but they should be easy to find. Grab yourself a straw and a cup of water. Fill the cup about a third of the way up. Now, place the straw in the cup, making sure the bottom of the straw doesn't touch the bottom. Inhale through your nose easily on a count of four. Then blow out through the straw, which is in the water. Again, make sure your straw isn't hitting the bottom of the cup, because you'll need room for the air to escape. And, just like your mother told you not to do at fancy restaurants, you'll be making air bubbles. Your goal is to make the bubbles come out in a smooth and even fashion. If you exhale too hard, the water will splash out of the cup and you'll make a mess (and upset Mom!). If you're too soft, you won't make a constant stream of bubbles.

After you've mastered this activity, you can add a hum to the exhale. This is called a semioccluded vocal tract exercise. Humming helps exercise and strengthen your vocal cords, and the breathing activity helps regulate the pressure against them.

## BUILDING VOCAL VARIETY AND EXPRESSION

### *Volume*

You'll immediately lose your audience if they can't hear you, but volume isn't only about whether your audience can hear you. It also helps you add emphasis, energy, interest, and meaning to your presentation. Varying your volume (even subtly) can be a very effective way to help keep your audience engaged and can add meaning. If you've ever seen written music for a musical or an opera, which is called the score, you might have noticed that the composer often puts notations or actual notes on how they want that portion of the music to be performed with respect to volume. You might see things like "*piano*," which means quietly; "*forte*," which means loud; or even "*fortissimo*," which is very loud. These notations are referred to as dynamics, and musicians and singers know they add color and emotion to the music. Good presenters vary their volume just the way a musician or singer would give the performance vocal color. Though in a presentation, you should always project enough to be heard by everyone in your audience.

### *Pace*

The optimal speaking pace for an English-speaking audience is about 125 to 150 words per minute. Speaking at a faster pace can work for or against you. When you do this, you're demanding that your audience work harder to keep up with you. A faster pace can keep the audience's level of concentration high and can be associated with passion and energy. If you're going fast because you're nervous, however, it will work against you. Ideally, you want to vary your pace—quick and energetic to communicate urgency, and slower to draw the audience's attention to a key point or takeaway. If you go too slow for an extended period, people will be bored. If you go too fast, people may lose details. Practice by picking a passage of about 130 words and time yourself. It should take around a minute. Then practice your presentation with this speed in mind.

## *Inflection and Tonality*

Tonality is the relationship between the high and low pitches in your voice, including where they occur, how often, and how frequently. People who we describe as monotone are not changing their pitch or their pace. Tonality and inflection are important because they impact meaning. They signal whether you sound sincere, insincere, or sarcastic. It's difficult, though, to *try* to change your pitch. The best way to work on varying your pitch is to think about emphasizing certain words or phrases to express their meaning. Look at the following example:

She works hard.

This simple three-word sentence could have three different connotations when spoken, just by where the speaker puts vocal weight. For instance, if the speaker emphasizes the word *she*, they are comparing this person to someone else. It could be that *he* doesn't work at all. If they emphasize *works*, they are making a distinction between working and doing something else. Maybe, she *plays* differently. Finally, if they emphasize *hard*, they are communicating that she puts in a lot of effort. She's not doing the bare minimum.

**She** works hard. (emphasis on the person)

She **works** hard. (emphasis on the fact that she works)

She works **hard**. (emphasis on how hard she works)

This is a much better approach to tonality than trying to change your pitch in the abstract. It makes for better meaning and more natural vocal variety. After you've written your script or speaker notes, go back and underline words that you want to emphasize because of their meaning in the phrase. This will give you great tonal variety.

## Avoid Upspeak

Upspeak—or high-rising terminal, as it is referred to by speech pathologists—is the tonal habit where every phrase sounds like a question. You may remember the sound of a "Valley girl" made popular by a 1980s song. When you end declarative sentences or phrases with a high pitch, the way we normally do with a question, you lose credibility and authority. Without getting feedback from someone or consciously listening for it, it can be tough to know if you're using this pattern. It's important to ask for feedback about this pattern if you suspect it has crept into your speaking habits.

## Articulation and Enunciation

Articulation is how we form sounds using our lips, teeth, tongue, and jaw. It refers to the clarity and expressiveness with which you speak. Enunciation refers to the physical sounds you make when you speak to convey that clarity and expressiveness. It's a technical distinction and one that we'll leave right here. The bottom line is, you want people to understand what you're saying. Here's a good way to think about it. You can wash your clothes and put them in the dryer. They come out clean and dry, but they probably have a few wrinkles. Or you can take them to the dry cleaners and have them come out clean and *crisp*. You don't want to sound garbled or have your words come out wrinkled; you want them to be clean and crisp. To do that, you need your articulators—the lips, teeth, tongue, and jaw—to be relaxed so you can direct them to the right place.

When I was in acting school, we had a speech class every day, and we started by getting our articulators going with tongue twisters. Here are just a few exercises (of which there are many) with which you can practice using your articulators. If you don't like these, grab a Dr. Seuss book and read it out loud. If you have children around, ask them to join you, and have some fun!

- "I need a box of biscuits; a box of mixed biscuits and a biscuit mixer."
- "Twixt this and six thick thistle sticks."
- "Red leather, yellow leather."
- "She sells seashells at the seashore."

## Filler Words

Filler words are the *ahs*, *ums*, *you knows*, *likes*, and *sos* that can be terribly distracting when we're listening to a presenter. They're sometimes called disfluencies. That's a good reminder that when we use too many filler words, we don't sound fluent. We look like we are not in command of our message and of our thinking. But we all use filler words now and then. In fact, sometimes the complete absence of an occasional filler word makes us sound unnatural. It's the overuse of filler words that undermines presenters. What does it take to avoid using too many filler words? It's a one-word answer: *discipline*. That's it. That's the most important part of ridding yourself of these nasty little intrusions to clarity. There are a few other tips that I'll share here, but you must commit yourself to the discipline of awareness if you want to improve.

Start by asking someone to count the number of filler words you use during a presentation practice session. Better yet, have them clap every time they hear a filler word. This will start to build your awareness. I've been a member of Toastmasters International for many years, and in each meeting, someone is assigned the role of the *ah* counter. They literally count the number of verbal fillers by category and report at the end of the meeting. A few meetings of hearing how many filler words are used get your attention. If you don't have anyone available to help you, use the voice recorder on your phone. If you really want to get fancy, use PowerPoint Speaker Coach or one of several speech apps on the market, such as LikeSo or Speako. They're great tools to build awareness.

There are also a few thoughts to help you deal with these verbal intruders. Try inhaling between phrases or sentences, where most fillers occur. When you inhale, you can't make a sound. Try it. By focusing on the inhale, you'll avoid the filler word, and you'll develop more consciousness of your use of fillers. Eliminating filler words takes practice, but it makes a big difference in your credibility and your ability to command attention.

**Pauses**

The final vocal technique we'll cover is the strategic use of pauses. Pauses are moments of brief silence in your presentation that are used to create interest or emphasize a point. You can pause momentarily before or after a significant moment in your presentation to underscore its weight. When you pause, you allow time for the audience to reflect, something that thoughtful business audiences value. An additional benefit to pausing is to allow time for the audience to ask a question. When they do, they are capitalizing on one of the most valuable aspects of presenting: live dialogue.

## Keep Your Voice Healthy

Speaking in public on a regular basis, and even speaking on the phone, can put enormous stress on your voice. It pays to keep your voice healthy by following a few simple guidelines. First, get plenty of rest. That's both the kind you get when you sleep and vocal rest, the kind you get when you're not using your voice. There's plenty of good advice on getting the right amount of quality sleep. Seven to eight hours per night for adults is advised. Good sleep hygiene keeps you mentally sharp, which is an important aspect of good presenting. Getting a good night's rest before an important presentation can be tough because of nerves. Doing a few relaxing breaths just before you're ready for bed can help you release some tension. Maybe even listen to music that relaxes you, or watch something on TV that's easy on your emotions.

There are also times when you'll want vocal rest. If you've been using your voice regularly, it may begin to get tired. A tired voice is hard to hear. If your voice is tired, it takes extra work to produce good sound. Giving yourself time to rest your voice isn't always easy when you have a busy schedule, so be intentional about finding time if your voice feels strained, hoarse, or tired.

## Drink Plenty of Water

One of the best things you can do for your voice is to stay hydrated. Pretty simple. One caution: if you drink too much water just before your presentation, you may need to run to the restroom at an inopportune time.

## Exercise

Keeping your body strong will help keep you healthy. Again, presenting is a physical activity! Your body and voice are your instruments. If you played the violin, you wouldn't leave it lying around after using it. You'd take pains to keep it clean and protected. You should do the same with your instruments. I shared the straw phonation exercises as a means of developing your breath. They are very good for caring for your voice as well. Because they don't put too much pressure on the vocal cords, they're ideal for gently activating the voice. Remember, you need your whole instrument to be fit for your big day of presenting.

You need to be fit to stand tall, breathe deeply, project your voice, and give your full energy to a presentation. Aerobic exercise like walking, cycling, or running is great. I also highly recommend yoga. It strengthens and tones the body. And with its focus on breathing, it's a perfect way to build your breathing capacity and stamina.

## Your Warm-Up Routine

All the exercises we've discussed make for a great practice regimen. Doing them every day will build strength and confidence. But they can also be incorporated into a warm-up routine on presentation day. A solid five-minute warm-up of voice and body will get you ready to take the stage. Start with these, and then create your own sequence.

Start with the body. A simple rag doll exercise is a great way to start, because it helps you relax. If you're tense just before your presentation, this exercise will help slow you down, release tensions, and get blood flowing to your brain. Simply bend at the waist, keeping your knees slightly bent, and allow your head, chest, and arms to hang freely to the ground. Gravity does all the work here. You don't need to do anything. Stay in this position for fifteen to thirty seconds, and just breathe easily. Then roll up slowly, and feel the relaxation of your body.

Next, do a few breathing exercises. I suggest two rounds of the 4–7–8 breath. Follow that up with three to four rounds of blowing out the candle, starting with a four-count inhale and exhale. After each successive round, add on a count. After that, try out some humming. This gets your vocal cords and your resonators (the facial bones, throat, and chest) warmed up and ready. You can simply start by inhaling to a count of four and exhaling all your breath while humming on a comfortable pitch. Do four to five rounds. Next, do the same humming, but this time after you start, open your mouth to make the vowel sound *ah.* This very open A vowel is easy to produce. You want to feel the same resonance with the *ah* as you did while humming. This is a gentle way to warm your voice and clear any mucous from your vocal folds. Finally, get those articulators working. Pick three or four of your favorite and most challenging tongue twisters, and go for it. I struggle with the *TH* sound, so "Twixt this and six thick thistle sticks" is always in my warm-up routine.

Allow yourself to have fun with your warm-ups. They will put you in an energized state, ready to bring your finely tuned instruments to the stage.

## Chapter 12 Key Takeaways

- Take the stage with purpose and confidence to make a strong first impression.
- Keep a straight, open posture to appear welcoming and confident.
- Use direct eye contact to connect with your audience and stay other oriented.
- Position yourself next to your visual aid, but don't read from it. Let the slides do the work.

- Use breathing exercises like 4-7-8, making the candle flicker, and straw breathing to relax and control your breathing muscles.
- Add vocal variety by carefully controlling your volume, pace, tonality, and inflection.
- Avoid filler words. Instead, use pauses to emphasize key points and control your thoughts.
- Keep your voice healthy by getting plenty of rest, drinking water, and exercising.
- Do a quick warm-up routine before presenting to relax your body and voice.

CHAPTER 13

# Ace Your Q and A

Treat objections as requests for further information.
—*Brian Tracy*

## The Role of Q and A

The question-and-answer period that accompanies public communication is one of the most difficult aspects of presenting, but it is one of the unique benefits of a live presentation that we've been discussing throughout this book. That's because you can immediately dialogue with the audience. You can clarify misunderstandings in the moment and offer supplemental facts, data, and reasons for your point of view. It's also a great way to build your credibility by demonstrating your poise under pressure and your fluency with the topic. Finally, it offers a great way to strengthen your connection to the audience as you continue to learn more about them throughout your presentation. Who wouldn't want that opportunity?

I'm sure it wouldn't surprise you to know that many speakers dread the question-and-answer period. And there are some good reasons for that. When I ask participants in our workshops what's most challenging or difficult about the question-and-answer period, their responses include, "Not being able to answer a question," "Not wanting to feel embarrassed," and "I don't want to look stupid." It makes sense. No one wants to feel caught on the spot like that. The question-and-answer period leaves you feeling vulnerable, but developing a few critical techniques can help you ace the Q and A and manage the anxiousness that comes with it.

## First, Understand Why Answering Questions and Objections Is So Tough

Presenting in high-stakes situations is difficult enough, but when a high-stakes question-and-answer period is involved, the level of difficulty increases. Let's look at some of the underlying stressors in a Q and A. First off, it feels like you're giving up control when you open the floor to questions. When you present, you're not only behind the wheel—you've also designed and built the car you're driving. But in the Q and A, you're no longer driving. The audience is, and it can be uncomfortable to move into the passenger seat. After all, they might drive like a novice, hesitating, swerving, or steering off the road completely. You just don't know.

### YOU MAY BE CHALLENGED

Depending on the situation, the "questions" you receive may be attempts to challenge your thinking or your research. Sales presentations, earnings calls, or venture pitches come to mind. Questioners have a variety of motives, and some are not always favorable to you. They may be looking to assert their point of view. You might feel that your knowledge, expertise, recommendation, or credibility is being called into question. You will be challenged. We see this in political press conferences and debates.

## FIGHT OR FLIGHT

Because of these Q and A dynamics, it is easy to feel a loss of control and be overcome with the very natural fight-or-flight response. When that happens (and it is unchecked), there are typically three types of responses—all detrimental to the presenter's credibility. One is defensiveness, where the speaker attempts to fight back. The second is an incoherent response, verbally running around in circles to evade or outmaneuver the "opponent." The third possibility is contentiousness. This happens when the speaker gets so upset at the nature of a question or having to take questions at all that they project disapproval. They may say curt or rude things or, in very rare circumstances, walk away and refuse to answer. Any of these responses negate all the hard work you've done preparing for and delivering your presentation. You lose any credibility you've established once you're on your heels.

**Questions are opportunities to uncover concerns, clarify a concept, and support a claim, or any other positive aspect of achieving your objective.**

The techniques we'll discuss here are designed to get you on, and keep you on, your toes. They are techniques associated with speaking impromptu or "off the cuff." Here I use the term to mean responding to questions that you're not given in advance. The techniques are also drawn from media training. Learning to speak effectively to the media is a valuable skill, and as presenters we can learn a great deal from the discipline. Learning a few techniques and practicing can make a big difference in your ability to handle the tough questions.

## Adjust Your Mindset

It begins with having the right mindset. Questions are opportunities to uncover concerns, clarify a concept, and support a claim or any other positive aspect of achieving your objective. You shouldn't internalize questions or objections posed to you or take them personally. Questions and objections shouldn't be seen as personal, even though it may feel like that at times. In most professional business settings, questions are the audience's way of exploring your thought process or presenting an opposing argument. Once you have the right mindset about questions, you'll feel more relaxed, which is critical to being able to slow your mind down and respond appropriately.

## Anticipate Questions

The best way to prepare is to anticipate the audience's questions. If you've done your homework, you already have a good sense of what the audience wants and needs. It's likely their questions will be centered on that. Think about your presentation, and honestly assess your vulnerability points. For example, if you're making a sales pitch and you know your product is more expensive than your competitors', you can be sure you'll get a question about cost. If you're presenting the timeline of a project that will take longer than your management expected, you need to prepare an answer for the inevitable question around timeline. I recommend that you write out a list of the questions you think you'll get and develop responses in advance.

## Know the Types of Questions You'll Get

If helping your audience make a decision is one of the primary reasons for giving a presentation, it's safe to say that the types of questions you'll get are those that any decision maker considers. Things like

"What **risks** are involved in accepting this proposal or using this product? Are we getting the best **value** for our investment? Is there are a way to accomplish our goals and spend less money? How difficult will it be to **implement** this solution, and how will it affect other parts of the organization?" And there are always questions asking for more detail. Thinking through the potential questions you'll get is the first step in effectively handling the Q and A session.

Let's use our characters as an example. Chuck is presenting to his own colleagues, who respect him and trust him. He's unlikely to get "gotcha" questions that are designed to capture a headline like he might get from a reporter or analyst. But he will get questions associated with risk and implementation. Because he's presenting a complex topic, there will likely be "How?" questions. "How does this fit into … ? How does that match … ?" He might be challenged. He needs to be ready to support and defend his conclusions. If Chuck has prepared well, this gives him a great opportunity to reassure his colleagues and provide the additional information they need to make decisions.

Amanda is facing a skeptical audience whose level of knowledge and trust in her and her product are still low. Because of that skepticism, she will get a lot of "Why?" questions. "Why should we trust you? Why should we adopt your solution?" Amanda's solution is also a new approach for her prospective customers. Due to that fact, there will be questions about implementation and the impact that this new approach will have on the entire organization.

If Cheryl opens the floor for questions, she will need to be ready for questions that could be emotionally charged. This is a difficult task for a presenter. As I mentioned earlier, when we feel challenged, the automatic fight-or-flight response kicks in and can throw us off balance. This might make Cheryl lose focus on the question. Let's explore the kind of questions she may get. It's probable that her audience will want to know "When?" "When can we expect to see change? When will things start improving for us?" She'll get "How?" questions too. "How will the new plan work?" And she'll also get some "What?" questions. "What will be different? What makes this plan better?"

These questions should remind you of the work from chapter 6, when you were building your presentation. The questions you get in the Q and A are the same questions you should ask yourself as you develop your presentation.

## Prepare Your Responses, and Master Your Messages

Now that you've considered the potential questions you'll get, write out your answers to each of them. Be sure to use strong language and simple words. When you write the answers out, it's like conducting a rehearsal. Your brain has *heard* the answers, and they become more accessible to you. Practice responding with your answers out loud. You may also want to create a slide for each question and have them ready as a backup as well. It takes discipline, but it will be extremely helpful in delivering crisp responses when the heat is on.

> The more you've prepared for questions in advance, the more confident you'll feel.

Author and sales expert Jeb Blount addresses this in his fantastic book *Objections:* "In emotionally tense situations, scripts free your mind, releasing you of the burden of worrying about what to say and putting you in complete control of the situation. A practiced script makes your voice intonation, speaking style, and flow sound confident, relaxed, authentic, and professional—even when your emotions are raging beneath the surface."[6] The more you've prepared for questions in advance, the more confident you'll feel. And feeling prepared is the best thing you can do to relieve any prepresentation nerves too.

## Learn How to Transition

There are times when a question may be off topic and answering would take the discussion in an unwanted direction. Transitioning back to the topic of the presentation is an important skill. I'm going to give you a few tips for how to do this as part of a simple process for handling Q and A.

First, **listen**. Once the audience member has the floor to ask a question, the first and most important thing you must do is carefully and actively listen. Focus only on what they are saying while the question is being asked. Do not start preparing your response in your head as they are speaking. When we let our mind wander to the response, we can miss important cues or words from the speaker. It is critical to be in the moment actively listening to the speaker.

Make eye contact with the speaker while they are talking. Watch for cues in their body language or tone that will help you understand their intent. Nod your head subtly as they are speaking to **acknowledge** what they are saying and indicate that you are listening. Use other nonverbal cues, like open body language to indicate that you are open and receptive to their question. This will also help you stay in a nondefensive frame of mind.

Wait for the questioner to finish the question before you answer. In addition to making them feel valued and heard, your goal in listening is to understand the "essence" or the "focal point" of the question. When you are listening for the essence of a question, you

---

6    Jeb Blount, *Objections: The Ultimate Guide for Mastering the Art and Science of Getting Past No* (United Kingdom: Wiley, 2018).

will be truly engaged with the speaker and will be able to respond more effectively.

You've listened carefully to the question, but before you respond, there is often an intermediate step that we call **clarify**. Not all audience members are good at asking questions. Sometimes what they are looking for is not apparent. Because you want to understand the true nature of the questioner's concern, you may need to ask questions to clarify your understanding before you respond. This is also a great way to uncover any hidden concerns or issues.

One way to do this is to use a simple paraphrase technique. For example, let's say an audience member says, "I'm worried the project will extend past the deadline." First, recognize this isn't phrased like a question, but there is definitely a question underneath. What you've got is a concern. You can use a paraphrase to help transition that concern into a question. This will allow you to answer their underlying question. You could say, "If I understood correctly, you would like to know more about how we will mitigate the risk of the timeline slipping. [pause] Is that correct?" Now you can provide a targeted response that addresses their underlying concern. You'll answer what you'll do to keep the timeline from slipping. Remember, paraphrasing is a reconfiguration of the question or statement, not a question about the question.

To create a paraphrase, identify the essence of the question or statement, and include a word like *what, why* or *how*. For example, "If I've understood correctly, you would like to know why we have selected these vendors," or "I'd like to confirm that you're interested in understanding how we hire our consultants."

Paraphrasing is also a good technique to give yourself a bit of time to think about your response while staying engaged with the questioner. The paraphrase acts as a buffer and can help absorb the shocking effect of a challenging question or objection and allow you to regain balance. It can also help build a connection with the questioner by showing that you are working to stay in sync with them. By paraphrasing their question, you show that you're listening and that you care about their critical perspective.

As you can tell by now, a Q and A session is rarely just questions and answers. There are some questions, sure. And concerns. Then there are just hard objections. This is another example where you need to ask a question to identify the underlying issue before responding. An audience member might say, "I don't like your timelines." Again, this isn't even a question, but remember, you're not the driver during the Q and A. You've got to adapt to this objection. Before responding, you really need to understand what the specific objection to the timeline is so that you can better address their concern.

This is such an important concept, and I urge you to pay attention to this point. It's very hard to resolve concerns that you don't understand. You're stabbing in the dark and unlikely to get to the true root of the problem. Just like a weed, if you don't get to the root, it's going to keep growing. You've got to get down to what my colleague, Kristina Hayes, calls "the solve zone" by taking the time to clarify their concern. If a questioner says, "I don't think your timeline dates are realistic," that doesn't tell us anything they think about the timeline except that it doesn't fit their expectations. Why is it unrealistic? Is it too long? Too short? Does it not have enough review time? What is their concern? Asking a simple question like "Can you share more about your concern with the timeline?" can help you answer more effectively and have a better shot of winning them over.

**Gracefully defer questions that are off topic.** Sometimes audience members have their own agendas and ask questions that don't relate to the topic at hand or are best left for a separate conversation. Let the questioner know you appreciate and acknowledge their concern but that the focus today is on the topic at hand. Assure them that they have a valid point that deserves a separate conversation or meeting.

## What If I Don't Know the Answers to the Question?

No one has all the answers, and there will inevitably come a time when you just don't know the answer. If you don't know the answer, simply admit that, and offer to get the answer. You could say something like "I don't have that information at the moment, but I will get back to you tomorrow with an answer to your question." Or, if you are presenting as a member of a group, you could redirect the question to the person who has the relevant expertise to answer the question. There is no reason whatsoever to make up an answer.

Presenters who handle questions well remain poised, are genuine, are agile, and are prepared.

## Chapter 13 Key Takeaways

- Q and A sessions are tough. If you perceive them as a threat, your emotions may take over and get in the way of providing a clear, succinct response.
- Having the right mindset about questions is the starting place for getting better at Q and A.
- Anticipate the questions you might get, and script out and rehearse them. This will boost your confidence and give you a better chance of providing an articulate response when the heat is on.

- Listen attentively, and demonstrate to the questioner that you are paying attention by using open body language and making eye contact.
- Use a paraphrase to make sure you and the questioner have a shared understanding of the question or issue.
- If a question is unclear, or if you sense a hidden concern, ask clarifying questions to get to the root of the issue.
- Your responses should be accurate and truthful. Don't make things up.

CHAPTER 14

# The Power of Virtual Presentations

You're on mute.

—*Every virtual meeting, every day*

The onset of COVID-19 has greatly accelerated the transformation that was already happening in the world of business communication. It shifted us to a world that mainly communicates through virtual methods. After March of 2020, I did one live training session and then attended almost no live meetings for over a year. I conducted plenty of workshops and, like you, attended many meetings, but they were all virtual. As a result of so much practice, I learned a few important things that I'd like to share with you. Mostly, I realized how much I love live, in-person settings ... but more on that later.

When you are presenting virtually, there are some important differences to consider. In virtual presentations, you lose some of the important channels for communicating meaning—mostly body language and proximity. Eye contact, which is one of the most important channels of nonverbal communication, changes significantly. Making eye contact in virtual presenting is a mixed bag. In some ways virtual presenters can make very direct eye contact by looking straight into the webcam. This requires that your camera be set at eye level and not too far away from you—about an arm's distance is ideal. You'll need proper lighting as well. When all these conditions have been met, you can make pretty good eye contact with your virtual audience.

What you can't do is look at one specific person and then move your glance to another so as to give your audience that very personal feeling that you are speaking directly to them. Fortunately for you, when your audience looks at their camera, or even at their screen, it appears as though they are looking directly at you. In many cases, you're getting a better look at them than you might in a large room or auditorium.

With these key differences in communication channels, more emphasis is put on your ability to engage the audience with your voice. You need more vocal energy and expressiveness. And you need better and more visuals. After all, when you present your slides in a virtual presentation, they are the size of a place mat, while your face is the size of a Post-it Note—unless you stop sharing your screen or "spotlight" yourself, which I recommend you occasionally do.

Before we discuss how visuals need to change, let's talk about a fundamental requirement of good virtual presenting—a good setup. There are three aspects of setup that you should master: lighting, sound, and framing.

## Lighting for Virtual Presentations

Your lighting makes a significant impact on the audience's experience when you are presenting virtually. If the room is too dark or the light is coming from the wrong direction, it can be very distracting. Your strongest source of light should be in front of you. If it's behind you—say, from a window—it will put you in shadow, and your audience won't get a good look at your facial expression. As you set up your presentation space, try to get natural light sources in front of you. If you don't have good natural light, or if you're presenting in the evening, you'll want to put a light source like a lamp behind your computer monitor. Inexpensive LED lights or ring lights are very common and available in most office supply stores or online. I recommend investing in one—you'll be surprised at the difference they make. If you work in a room with overhead fluorescent lights, consider turning them off; they too can cast unattractive shadows.

## The Importance of Good Sound

Studies show that 60 percent of the impression a video makes on its viewer is based on the quality of the sound. I think we can extrapolate from this that your sound quality really matters. Most computers' built-in microphones won't give you the sound quality you need to make it a more pleasing listening experience for your audience. There are many options for improving your sound in a virtual setting. They range from high-end USB microphones to using your Bluetooth earbuds. Also, take into consideration the sound dynamics of the room. If you're presenting from a room that doesn't have carpet or much furniture to absorb some of the sound, you may get an echo. I'm not suggesting you redecorate your house for a presentation, but if you have a choice of rooms, one with less echo (and good lighting) would be best.

## Looking Good on Camera

Spend some time adjusting the zoom and angle of the camera so that you're well centered in the frame and so that you aren't too close or too far away. Again, you want to be about an arm's distance from the camera. Frame yourself so the audience can see all of your head and about halfway between your shoulders and elbows. This allows them to see your expressions well without your being just a face. It also avoids showing your desk, which can be cluttered for some folks. You want the camera height to be set at eye level. You might need to change your camera settings for color, contrast, or brightness—some cameras have more controls than others, but very likely you will be able to at least adjust the brightness.

Your goal is to look as natural as possible. What you wear also makes a difference. Cameras don't do well with patterns. Stripes, plaids, and busy prints aren't going to do as well on camera as a solid color. You will also want to avoid large, shiny jewelry that can distract or glare. Be conscious of your posture. You want to sit up straight and tall, and be careful of slouching or leaning back too far. A chair that doesn't rock or swivel and supports good posture can be helpful. Be careful of your body movements—not too much, as this can be distracting. In general, move and gesture less than you would in an in-person presentation.

> **Your goal is to look as natural as possible.**

## Visuals

When you are standing in front of an audience delivering a meaningful message in an engaging way, almost nothing you put on a screen will be as interesting to watch as you. This just isn't the case virtually. As I mentioned earlier, your audience will be seeing a big screen and a little you. Your visuals must be engaging. While the elements we covered in chapter 10 still pertain, there are a few additional considerations. When audiences watch screens today, they've been conditioned by movies, YouTube, and even Facebook and Instagram to expect lots of visual action—cuts, fades, animation, and camera movement. As a virtual presenter, you need to simulate that visual action. This means more slides, more animation, and more transitions. While this will help you engage your audience, it's not a license for meaningless images, superfluous motion, or choppy transitions.

Virtual presenting is tough, but when you incorporate some of these simple techniques, you'll have a better chance of keeping your audience focused on what you have to say and not their email.

> **Your audience will be seeing a big screen and a little you.**

## Chapter 14 Key Takeaways

- Virtual presenting is here to stay. Make sure you set up your environment with good lighting, sound, and camera position to make your onscreen presence powerful.
- The camera doesn't like stripes, checks, and patterns. Wear more solid colors when presenting virtually.
- Enhanced vocal energy helps you make an emotional connection and make up for some of the communication channels that are diminished in virtual presentations.
- Use more motion and animation on your slides to keep your audience engaged.

# The Last Word

A great presentation is like a lighthouse shining through a dense fog. It can provide a path forward, warn of impending danger, cut through organizational noise, and even be a beacon of hope. It takes both discipline and creativity to put together a clear and meaningful message. It takes even more to deliver it in a compelling way. When you do, you will be helping your audience—maybe by helping them make a better decision, or learn a new skill, or plan for the future. Whatever it is for *your* audience, the hard work you have done will have been worth all the effort. There is power in presentation. Use it well.

# Acknowledgments

When I first met my wife, I told her how much I loved performing as a Broadway actor. In typical fashion, she said, "Who wouldn't love a job that when you finish your day's work, people stand and clap for you?" She was right. Except for professional sports, it's hard to imagine any other profession where you get so much acknowledgment of your work—right when you finish. I mean, when was the last time you walked out of the office to cheers?

While it was certainly thrilling to hear that applause, the truth is, there were so many unseen and unacknowledged players who made the onstage performance possible. In the theater they are collectively referred to as "the crew." They are the stagehands, lighting professionals, sound engineers, wardrobe pros, makeup artists, orchestra musicians, and so many more great professionals. We take the bows, but they deserve just as much credit. So, it is with great humility that I share my gratitude with the wonderful "crew" that helped me with this endeavor.

Many thanks to all the amazing professionals I've had the opportunity to have as participants and partners in countless workshops and training programs. I have learned so much from you. Your passion for leading, selling, and building teams has inspired me, and I am grateful to have had the opportunity to work with you. A special bow to the many great learning and development professionals I worked with: John Nasser, Jim Phelan, Amie Lyn Fitzpatrick, Greg Megowan, Amber Daugherty, Andy Norris, Karen Clement, Michael Ratican, Laura Last, Charlie Gardner, Tracy Turley, Bill Lutz, Lloyd Hilton, and Molly Weene.

Thank you to Vital Talent's great partner and my friends at 4th Down Solutions—Brett Howell and James Bodaglio—your vision is transforming how we do organizational learning. It's also very gratifying to see leaders really put the ideas we write about into action. I've seen that firsthand with leaders like Tamara Ziegler, John Reeves, and Eric Braverman. I love watching you at work!

I was lucky when I made the transition from the stage to the corporate world to have Larry Brown as my role model. Thank you, Larry, for taking me under your wing and giving me the chance to lead.

I was also fortunate to get to work for Dr. Sam Shriver. When it comes to training presentations, no one is better. Thank you, Sam and Maureen, for the opportunity to work alongside you and the team at the Center for Leadership Studies.

This book would never have been possible without all the help I received from some very talented young professionals, especially Taylor De La Pena, whose writing and organizing skills helped bring this idea to life. Thank you so much Taylor. I was also fortunate to have Taylor Holst, Alex Re, and our associate editor at Vital Talent, Rachel Melnotte, help with research. I am so impressed with how smart all of you are! Thank you also to the great team at Advantage Books—Steve, Connor, Harper, Laura, and Megan. You have been so patient with me, and I really appreciate it.

Sometimes it's dark in the wings of the theater, and you need someone to shine a light to help you find the entrance to the stage. Shining the light for me are David Mantica, my trusted coach and friend, and Dr. Charles Browning, whose counsel and guidance have shed so much light in some places I really needed it. Thank you, Dr. B.

I have an awesome team at Vital Talent. I know my job is to support them, but they give back more than they get. Kathleen Kelley, Alyssa D'Avanzo, Rachel Melnotte, Liz Earnhardt and Robert Gibney—you guys rock. Thank you for your commitment to each other and to Vital.

Vital Talent would not exist without two of the most talented learning and development professionals in the business, Todd Campbell and Kristina Hayes. You are amazing, and I am so grateful for all the help and support you have given me over the years. It is such a joy to work with you.

Throughout every crazy endeavor in my life, and there have been many, my parents, brothers, and sister have been there for me, encouraging me, strengthening me, and reminding me of what matters most in life. Mom, Joe, Janine, and Rob, you are the best. I love you. I wish Dad were here for this.

For the past thirty years I've had the joy of being accompanied on this amazing journey by my wife, Carrie, and twenty-eight of those years with our son, Tyler. Tyler, your kindness and intelligence inspire me. You have given me more than you can imagine. Carrie, you are my treasure. Thank you for never giving up on all my ideas and for helping me achieve my dreams. How you've made it all these years with a combination of Ralph Kramden, Felix Unger, and Frasier Crane, I'll never know, but please don't stop!

Finally, I thank God, Father, Son, and Holy Spirit, for all the blessings you have bestowed on me, everyone mentioned above, and so much more.

CPSIA information can be obtained
at www.ICGtesting.com
Printed in the USA
BVHW010931071022
648918BV00010B/383